Profit by Design

THE Blueprint to Successfully Scale Your Business
and Regain Your Freedom

Profit by Design

THE Blueprint to Successfully Scale Your Business and Regain Your Freedom

John Waters

Waters Business Consulting Group

HEALY QUINN
PUBLISHERS

Copyright © 2022 John Waters

This book is based on true and real-life experiences. These are my memories, from my perspective, and I have tried to represent events as faithfully as possible. The information in this book was correct at the time of publication, but the Author does not assume any liability for loss or damage caused by errors or omissions.

To request permissions, or schedule engagements, contact the author at jwaters@watersbusinessconsulting.com. For order or bulk purchases of this book. Please write jwaters@watersbusinessconsulting.com.

Library of Congress Control Number: 2021931418
Healy Quinn Publishers, West Linn, Oregon
Edited by Meghan Wier; Cover design by Erin Haynes
Waters, John
        Profit by Design: THE Blueprint to Successfully Scale Your Business and Regain Your Freedom

ISBN: 978-1-7362041-0-8
ISBN: 978-1-7362041-1-5

Dedication

This book is dedicated to the unique individuals who had the courage to step out in faith and start their business, and to those who may have bought a business, or dream and aspire to become an entrepreneur.

The risk of failure is significant and well-documented, so the challenges you have, or will encounter in starting and/or growing a business can be daunting, frustrating, and discouraging. However, I encourage you to persevere with your purpose, passion, and dream because it is your grit, faith and perseverance that will help you succeed.

When you succeed, as you are sure to do with grit and solid plan, you will enjoy the fruits of victory. You will find joy and satisfaction in your accomplishments, including the hoped-for financial success and freedom that motivated you to begin your journey as an entrepreneur in the first place. Take action! Action trumps everything!

Finally, to my children, Shea, Grant, and Ella, you inspired me when I encountered challenges and found myself discouraged and wanting to give up. I knew you were watching, so I persevered and so will you in your life with your dreams in business, your career, and your relationships. Commit to never giving up, to finishing and do your best no matter the difficulties, and you will always know you succeeded regardless of the outcome. Go get your dreams!

For my faith in God that keeps me grounded, humbled, balanced, focused, and always striving to improve, and to know my true purpose and identity.

Acknowledgments

When I began to write **Profit by Design**, it started out as an eBook. As the book took shape, my team encouraged me to continue improving on each chapter. I am blessed and thankful to these people who supported me and encouraged me through this process and in life;

My father, for his example of a work ethic and showing me that hard work is required to become a successful entrepreneur.

My mother, for always challenging my core values and encouraging me to stay true to myself.

My six brothers and sisters, for providing me the opportunity to grow despite my past failures and shortcomings, and to stretch myself to be the man I am today.

To all my close friends and family, for loving me despite my past challenges and always encouraging me.

Kevin McCarthy, my good friend and mentor with this project, my keynote speeches, and my lifetime encounters. Thank you for visiting me when I needed a friend, for paving the way with your book and keynote, and for encouraging and challenging me to commit. Your support and guidance have been invaluable, and you help me more than you know. Thank you.

Meghan Wier, my manuscript writer and editor. Thank you for bringing meaningful content and interest to each chapter and client stories so the book is an easier and more enjoyable read. You are gifted.

Paul Weathers, my senior consultant and friend. Thank you for helping me bring structure to our *Profit by Design* methodology so that each chapter builds on the previous and provides order, clarity, and direction. You are exceptional in simplifying the complex and instrumental in helping to bring order to this book and our clients' businesses.

Erin Haynes, for being available for weekly Zoom calls to review progress on this book and your help creating the book cover. You are always a support and a positive light to us all, and I am grateful for having you on our team and working together for the past seven years.

My Men@Work and Truth@Work leadership groups, for encouraging me and holding me accountable for becoming a better man and leader. Thank you to Rick Richards, Paul Pastore, Dave Hart, and others, along with Kelly Cook, Brent Byerly, James Peacock, Mark Miller, and Dave Kotter, for your examples. You are all men I admire and can count on!

My clients, for providing me the opportunity to continue to learn and grow as we help each of you and your teams grow your business, and for challenging me to stretch myself so I can better serve you. Without your business and trust, I could not finance this project, nor would the book be enriched with the case studies and stories that provide relevant examples for each chapter. Thank you for the opportunity to serve all of you!

For my team of Senior Consultants, Client Project Coordinators, Analysts, and Support, for without them I would not have the bandwidth to undertake this project. Thank you for your dedication to this project and our methodology to help businesses scale successfully. Thank you, Jack Weiss, Dominic Randazzo, Jordan Jasper, John Gillen, Paul Jackson, and Will Zajic.

I am honored and blessed to work with each of you as we help our clients improve and scale their business so that they can earn more income, work less, and live out their purpose in life.

Table of Contents

Introduction

Profit by Design is a success methodology developed by John Waters of **Waters Business Consulting Group**. The methodologies and approaches used are the culmination of 35 years of John's business experience in various industries, coupled with his research, mentoring, failures and successes in 9 different businesses of his own, and hundreds of client businesses over the years. John has summarized his approach into simplified methodologies applicable to any business and any stage in the business life cycle. Now, these are available to you and your business. If implemented, the **Profit by Design Methodology** will have a profound and long-lasting impact on the success of your business and the overall quality of your life, and as a leader.

In this book, we're going to outline the **10 Steps Towards Growing (and Scaling) Your Business**. We have broken this book into 10 main chapters, one for each of the steps, as well as included real-life case studies from our practice. Through our own businesses, and the business coaching and consulting of over hundreds of organizations, we have developed this program that will help you understand, grow and even sell your company with success! We look forward to sharing our blueprint and working with you to help you grow your business.

10 Steps Towards Growing Your Business

1. Vision Casting
2. Financial Forecasts
3. Organizational Modeling
4. People / Leadership Positioning
5. Operational Workflows
6. Marketing Strategies
7. Track/Measure/Refine Metrics
8. Leverage Customer Feedback
9. Customer Retention Strategies
10. Exit Planning

We built these methodologies to help small-to-medium sized business owners scale their organizations, improve their sales, and take their companies to the next level. This process has been refined in over 3 decades of working in and with multiple businesses and industries. The principles are universal, but the methodologies of **Profit by Design** are specific to what works most effectively for the hundreds of businesses and clients that have been coached through this comprehensive process.

You are welcome to read this book cover-to-cover, or use it as a workbook, (or both) as each step builds upon the next. We hope you carefully consider the questions asked and add notes to be discussed as you work through these steps for your own business.

Finally, as with any information and learning, these methodologies only work if they are implemented. **Your success is dependent on action!**

Chapter 1

Vision Casting

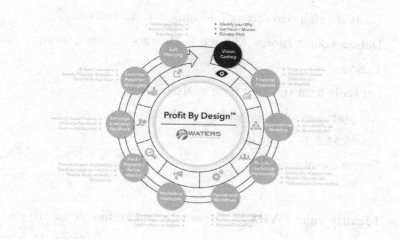

Vision Casting is about identifying what your "WHY's" are. *Why did you start a business? What are your dreams, vision, and mission?* Vision Casting allows the business owner to understand their own role in a business, as well as to motivate employees to invest in the organization's future. Vision Casting also provides employees with the opportunity to succeed in their own roles within an organization, by identifying and achieving long-term goals which advance the health of a company. A Vision is instrumental to establishing a culture that attracts and retains high performing talent. A Vision helps your customers/clients to identify with your core purpose to determine if it aligns with their fundamental purpose and objectives.

Vision Casting includes:

- Identifying your "WHY?"
- What are your real dreams? – Think outside the box.
- Define your Vision / Mission – Dreams are the precursor to your Vision.
- Set short-term and long-term goals.
- Are your goals aligned with your Vision?
- Set "S.M.A.R.T." goals.
- Create elevator pitch.

Identify your "WHY." We want to understand: *What are your real dreams? What is it that motivates you to do what you're doing?* You want to think outside of the box to identify that real emotional drive for growing your business and define your vision and mission. Ultimately, those things that you dreamed about when you decided to start your own business are what I call the precursor to your Vision. How did you get the idea or spark that made you begin the business journey in the first place?

When you set short-term and long-term goals, you must make sure that your goals are aligned with your Vision. We've all heard of SMART goals, but this is where you want to establish those to be <u>Specific</u>, <u>Measurable,</u> <u>Aligned</u> with your core values, <u>Realistic</u> and <u>Time</u> sensitive. **What are your goals, do they align with your Vision, and are they SMART?**

Think of your Vision or Vision Statement as an outline of what your business would like to ultimately achieve and gives purpose to the existence of your organization. A good Vision Statement should be short, simple, specific to your business, and clear. It should also have some energy and passion. The next step is to create an **elevator pitch**. An elevator pitch is a short description of an idea, product or company that explains the concept in a quick and easily understood way. This all falls into the **Vision Casting** heading, and we find that there are several challenging points for a lot of clients at the phase. Many have reported that they have trouble getting started and outlining the goals of their business to staff. An elevator pitch "packages" the business "why" and "what" for your clients and staff. Developing a 30-second explanation of what you do and why, aligns all employees to start from the same place.

Here is a good example of elevator pitch from Toyota USA:

Mission: *To attract and attain customers with high-value products and services and the most satisfying ownership experience in America.*

Vision: *To be the most successful and respected car company in America.*

Here is another good example of elevator pitch from Southwest Airlines:

Mission: *The mission of Southwest Airlines is dedication to the highest quality of customer service delivered with a sense of warmth, friendliness, individual pride, and company spirit.*

Vision: *To become the world's most loved, most flown, and most profitable.*

As you can see, these Mission and Vision Statements –state their "why" very well. It gives concrete information and says what they do and why—and it says so in a paragraph or less! Your elevator pitch needs to do the same and will simplify your messaging.

Ultimately, if a business owner is unable to establish a Vision that they can manifest, they will experience serious setbacks when adversity strikes or they will fail because they don't have the "why" or Vision to remain focused and overcome challenges. Essentially, they can't establish the goals because they don't have the Vision to do so. They don't know where to start and they don't know how to give direction to their staff. They can't figure out how to set goals, and they're chasing <u>too many</u> goals. This is a very common challenge, one that I have faced over the years. But it can be overcome.

Business owners often need help setting goals. This includes their own personal goals, the business and their team goals. When someone can't connect the Vision they have for their company with their goals, we work with them, giving them the tried-and-true tools that have worked for hundreds of businesses before them. Once the business owner has a template for creating goals s/he is able to begin the process.

So often, what we find is that the business owner has some sort of a dream or an idea. Then this dream develops into a Vision, Mission and goals. From the goals, we begin to develop the strategies to achieve the goals and by achieving the goals, they achieve their vision. As we move down the first methodology, the Vision and Mission all begins to come together, and we are able to shift to develop strategies. For most businesses, strategy is ultimately tied to finances and financial forecasting as well as organizational development tied to these financial objectives and is the next step in our methodology.

Vision Casting Client Spotlight:
Commercial HVAC Company

From Rudderless Ship to Robust Enterprise

Recently, we started working with the owner of a rapidly growing Commercial HVAC Company in Arizona. Through strong and visionary leadership, the company had established itself as a profitable high quality HVAC company in the Phoenix metropolitan Valley Area. Beneath the façade of the growth and profitability, the owner was facing burnout. On some days, he felt like he was the captain of a rudderless ship running awry. It was the kind of feeling you experience when you are losing control of your vehicle in on a slippery surface.

At the time, there were no defined processes, plans, directives, standards operating procedures, and a clear sense of direction of the business. In the owner's defense this is not unique to him. Over the years, we have come to observe this scenario whenever growth outpaces management's agility in keeping up with the demands of their time. As a result of the fluid situation, the CEO and President experienced some trepidation as well as tribulations while shaping a better tomorrow.

Based on our assessment, one of the biggest challenges that affected leadership and employees was the lack of an Organization Structure. That issue plagued them from the start, like is the case with many ups. They also lacked defined roles and responsibilities. This led to many employees wearing different hats. While this is not entirely alien, at Fiat, this became an impediment to growth because some employees were stepping on each other's toes, thereby breeding animosity, infighting and bickering.

The owner started out by outlining what he called the "virtues" he wanted to model himself and as part of his culture. The virtues he and his team established are:

- **Justice.** In asking how this fits into the vision and mission, it was noted that Fiat needs to be fair and equitable to everyone, including internally with employees and staff and externally with customers. Fiat needs to continually ask themselves if they are being fair to customers and their needs.

- **Charity.** This fits into the mission much as justice does. A life of justice and fairness cannot be achieved without charity. For example, Fiat should be charitable even if someone is a debtor. Everyone needs a chance.

- **Prudence.** This fits into the mission as it pertains to all resources, even beyond money. Prudence is the best use or wisest interaction with anything, including time and decision making on sensitive employee or customer issues.

- **Fortitude.** Fiat does not believe in giving up. The owner tries to encourage people to never give up because the answer is always around the corner if one is willing to look for it. The team noted a part of fortitude is being humble and knowing when to ask for help, and when to defend what is right.

In consultations with the owner, he often expressed concerns and frustrations with what he termed, "the lack of a solid business plan, strategic plan and marketing plan – equals no vision no direction." In order to redress that situation, we helped them to design a roadmap or what we call "Workflow Process Map" This included an Organization Chart, and a Profit by Design Financial Model. Each of these was designed to further strengthen processes and procedures. Above all, the goal was to help them have a firm grip on the rudder of their ship by providing greater clarity on the roles/direction of the business. There is ample evidence that some of these changes have started yielding fruit. The proof, they say is in the pudding. In 2020, the company surpassed their revenue goal by over 25%. Working with this partner has taught us, an invaluable lesson: where the is no destination, there is no roadmap.

After multiple collaborative sessions with our client, and an outstanding effort with their team and ours openly sharing our thoughts and challenging each other, we formalized their Vision and Mission Statements as follows:

Mission Statement:

Providing comfort, reliability, and peace of mind, we serve and educate communities by igniting, lifting, and inspiring the human spirit of our clients and employees through personal and professional development.

Vision Statement:

Exceptional people influencing lives, impacting communities through exceptional services.

Now, our client is energized, focused, and enthused with building their culture around their Vision and Mission, and developing a strategic recruiting, training and retention plan that integrates different parts of the company. Our consultation with this client continues to grow stronger, one year after we initially stated this relationship. Recently, we started working on a Training Program for Technicians, helping them design Career Paths ranging from 0-5 years. This will help the company to recruit, train, retain quality technicians to reduce attrition and seasonal fluctuations. Additionally, we have developed an analysis that determines the actual performance expectations for technicians to break even and generate a profit for the business or what we call REI (Return on Employee Investment.

Ultimately, this will help management to control productivity and to generate a better return on investment for the business. To further boost productivity, we are helping the client to pair-up employee performance with an incentives program that will boost the performance of technicians who have a full grasp and understanding of established KPI's necessary to meet the ROI or REI. So far, we have made considerable progress in setting up business processes and procedures. As our relationship continues to evolve, we are in the process of assisting the owner in developing a framework and plan for his long-term vision of selling the company. Although the project started out like a sprint, it has evolved into a marathon with many markers of success.

Vision Casting Client Spotlight:
Commercial Mortgage Broker

We have a client who does commercial lending, and he is a great example of Vision Casting done well. I have worked with him for almost 3 years now, but he is very clear on identifying what his "why" is. This client knows what he wants to pursue and can drill back into his target, goals, the strategies and the tactics in order to get there. I have worked with him to help implement his Vision and Mission, and he is one of the best leaders that I have seen in executing and ensuring that everything that he does is filtered through his Vision, Mission and his goals. I will share this with you, because I feel that he has a powerful laser-focused Mission, and as a result, his organization thrives. This client's purpose and "why" they exist as a company is stated below.

To Please God by seeking 3 key areas:

- Peace of mind.
- Place the Gospel.
- Protect the poor and disenfranchised.

This commercial lender carries this out in his business without fail, so the people he hires know what's important to him and the business. He believes that he is there to generate revenue and earn an income to provide for his family and for others, but also to use those resources to share the Gospel message of hope. This may not resonate with you, but that is what is important to him. He has his core convictions, and uses an acronym called CHASE:

C - Commitment to follow the Christ model and put others as more important than yourself.

H - Honesty doesn't matter the consequences, stand firm.

A - Apply candid but gracious feedback.

S - Simplify the process.

E - Excel by finishing where they want to be.

Key things the client speaks of all the time:

- He wants to <u>be proactive</u> in identifying and preventing potential future problems. He wants to be proactive with his clients as they are managing the loan process because it can get very shaky and then all of a sudden, the underwriter can pull or it's cancelled. Being proactive can save the process from falling apart.
- He wants to <u>provide confidence</u> to his clients and have full trust that he is seeking the client's best interest.
- He has found <u>a niche,</u> providing a proactive process which will provide confidence of execution.

These are some core components of their Vision/Mission. To everyone involved in this company, their Vision and Mission are clear and the benefit of that is that all the hires that I have helped the owner interview and qualify are filtered through this process. In fact, everything they do is filtered through this process. The company owner regularly has events where he is sharing inspirational faith-based stories. He owns his Vision and Mission, and he serves the poor as part of that because that is what he feels he is called to do. I have been involved in some of these programs with the client, and I have witnessed his commitment to his Vision and Mission, and not just one time a year; he does this probably 7 or 8 times a year! He does some major events, including fundraising for the poor, and he's recently doing one called **Hope from Fear**. He practices what he preaches. It is because everything is filtered through his Vision, and he cast that Vision, (clearly establishing that Mission), his business is profitable, and his employees aligned and dedicated. He regularly reviews Mission, Vision and goals with all employees as well as other key metrics and expectations. His business has thrived, and he is fulfilled in his personal and business goals.

That is a great example of an individual who cast a Vision and lives it out, and as a result is successful. But beyond the success of the company, he has personal success as a leader in the community, as a husband, father and leader in his church. Since he has a personal commitment, employees want to be engaged and they want growth opportunities, and they want their work to matter–and in this case it absolutely does!

Chapter 2
Financial Forecasts

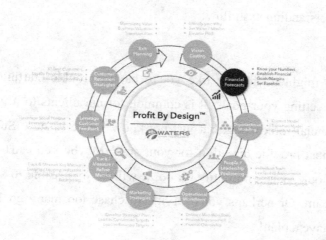

A **Financial Forecast** is an estimate of future financial outcomes for a company and is a next important step following Vision Casting. This step follows the direction of the Vision and gives you objective targets and helps to develop a roadmap to confidently advance your business forward to meet your goals based on measuring your actual financial results against your financial forecast model.

A Financial Forecasts includes:

- Knowing your numbers.
- Establishing financial goals.
- Understanding your margins.
- Analyzing your trends to establish a baseline.

- Using transactions to forecast future revenues vs. growth based on percentages.
- Defining staff and overhead required to achieve financial goals to establish metrics.
- Understanding cash flow.

You might be feeling like you're having trouble starting, creating outlines and setting your goals. It is common for our clients to want to work through financial forecasting, but just not know where to start. Success will mean you must provide direction for your staff. Maybe you can't figure out how to set your goals, and until you do, it will be impossible to share them with your team. Or perhaps you're trying to chase too many goals! Do not worry. We have a plan!

As we shift into the first area of ideal strategies, what I look at when I'm working with a client are the financial details. The reason we start with financial numbers is to analyze the data based on past trends. The numbers are objective and tell us a clear picture of where you've been, without emotion. The numbers tell us a true story of a business's performance.

We review the financial history of the organization, and we usually look at the last two or three years to establish a trend with Revenue, average dollars per transaction, Cost of Goods, Gross Margins, Operating Overhead and Net Operating Income. From there, we can determine where we anticipate the business is going based on past trends. Past trends are the best predictor of the future performance of the organization.

However, we find our clients are often looking for growth– something that goes above and beyond the past performance. That means doing things differently, and determining how we can leverage opportunities, streamline operations and build a team. For example, if you're doing $5 million and you want to grow to $10 million, you will need to look at not just growing gross revenue 100%, but also growing in terms of transactions over a period of time since transactions are how businesses monetize their services or product versus growing by a percentage. By determining growth in terms of transactions, it requires our clients to consider where they will market to customers in order to obtain these transactions.

In short, it's important to know what your numbers are, and establish the financial goals of the business for us to help you get there.

An example: If you were doing $5 million a year in gross revenue and you want to get to $10 million, I would review your numbers and ask "over what period of time?" Depending on the circumstances, that may be obtainable in three years, four years, or five years. The plan to get there will look differently depending on the time horizon, available capital, people, execution, strategies and opportunities, etc. I tell our clients that if you have a viable, legitimate legal business with a market for your product and services, we can guarantee growth. Now, how much growth will depend on available resources as noted above. So, knowing that, if you have capital and human resources with a strategic plan, it's just a matter of time and resources executed, to get you to your growth objectives.

Once we understand what your revenue goals are, then we want to look at your margins. This includes your actual gross margins and your net margins. **Margin** refers to the difference between selling price and the seller's variable costs for the goods or services on sale. Margins come out of your direct costs associated with driving revenue which are typically your labor and materials. We want to establish a baseline for how you've been performing and then understand what your current cash flow is. The Financial Forecast then allows us to be very objective about how we're going to achieve those numbers. We look at the financial statements or P&L (profit loss statements) to determine what's driving your revenue, what your cost of goods are, your gross margins and your net profit so that we can develop a strategy to grow and improve these financial metrics.

The next step is to determine where you'd like to see improvement in those financial metrics, and we look at how you're managing your business. Finally, we incorporate our fees into that structure to make sure that our cost is accounted for as part of the operation so that we ensure a real return on investment.

Many of the clients that we deal with are not sure how to develop a forecast or how to properly plan. They don't understand what their sales pipeline looks like, or their schedule of production or services. They're not sure what numbers are important to their business in terms of the key metrics to monitor. Many times, what we have found is that our clients are not sure when and how to grow. If you have too many employees, you are inefficient. There is cost. But if you don't have enough employees, you can't grow. We work to help you with the strategy so that you can execute with your team and capital…realizing that you can't scale a business without people. Many of our clients ask; "when do I hire the people to support my growth?" With the Forecast Model, we track actual performance trends to determine the best timing for investment into hiring employees and adding to infrastructure to grow. There is a cost to growth because you must hire people in order to grow. People are an investment. Without people, growth is not possible.

One thing to note is that often, I'll meet with a client, and they may be talking about <u>gross profit</u> but they're referring to <u>net profit</u>. Understanding the words, and the financial principles behind them will heighten your ability to manage and improve the finances of the business. It will also help you understand your cost of doing business.

Driving revenues is important. I can't tell you the number of businesses that talk about top line growth in revenue. Don't get me wrong, revenue is important. But the number that really matters is **gross profit margin**. (Note: <u>gross profit</u> is typically known as the dollar amount, <u>gross margin</u> is known as a percent of that dollar amount.) Using gross profit margin (GPM), is the margin after direct costs or cost of sales is deducted from your revenue. Deducting direct costs and overhead expenses from your revenue are known as **net operating income**. You could have a company doing $10 million and making 15% gross profit. However if you're operating overhead is 20% you're at a net loss of -5% (15% Gross Profit Margin less 20% Operating Overhead Expenses = - 5%).

Getting to profitability starts with pricing your product or service with the right **gross profit margins**. Without the price including the right profit margin, you can't generate the gross profit dollars to scale and do so profitably. So, one of the priorities that we really focus on with our clients, is how you structure your business in terms of managing your **direct costs**, (the labor and materials costs that go to driving that top line number), and then making sure you get your operational overhead in line so that you generate a positive net operating income which allows you to cash flow your business. The numbers are very critical at this stage because they establish our baseline metrics. They allow us to measure and determine the type and volume of transactions that are going to feed the growth. We don't build a financial model without doing any of this. We develop this using financial models based on our financial analysis, and the growth is not based on some arbitrary percentage. We forecast growth of revenue based on the size and volume of transactions that drive that revenue. You must develop a way that's realistic—no business grows revenue without doing transactions, and we calculate the number of transactions based on your average transaction dollar amount per transaction. These transactions will determine the infrastructure and people required to scale.

Let's look at the example. You want your business to go from $5 million to $10 million in annual revenue. It is not simply a matter of percentage growth, because it wouldn't be accurate. You want to look at what number of transactions historically have been growing your business, and what number will be driving that growth based on the average dollar per transaction. Admittedly, that stuff can tend to be a bit dry for some people, but the beauty with the numbers, is they give us very hard data to start building the rest of the profit by design model, and from there we can determine the people, the workflow, the marketing, some of the more engaging and exciting strategies required to support those transactions…the fun stuff!

Often when we start to work with a client. The first thing they say is *"I want to grow top line revenue. I need more sales."* Well, it may not be the sales you need to address. In fact, you may have the opportunities coming in, but you're not <u>converting</u> them. So it may be a customer or client conversion issue. The numbers will tell us that—and the more we dive into the numbers, the more information we have to make decisions on where we're going to build the strategies to grow the business. So that's why we start with analyzing the numbers!

When we prepare to grow a business, there are four key components that are necessary. You've got to have **people**, the **strategy**, the **ability to execute** that strategy and **capital**. You can't execute the strategy without the people, nor the capital. People become incredibly important to growing a business. You can have a building and all the equipment to manufacture the best automobile or the best widget, but it takes people to execute. So, we model out what the organization looks like today, and what it will look like when it grows from $5 million to $10 million using the financial forecast and an organization chart.

Let me explain why people are key to your growth. If I were to ask you, *"How many employees do you currently have?"* You might tell me, *"Today, we've got 25 employees, and these are the different roles, etc..."* That is great, and we're going to help you put those positions in an organizational structure if you don't already have one. (Some businesses do and some don't.)

An organizational structure helps you get a clear picture of who your team is, and what their respective role is and their financial cost and impact on revenue to the business. This helps you to determine the employee's ROEI (Return On Employee Investment). It also provides detail and structure regarding the responsibilities and roles that will help you to manage and grow the business. The reason that's important is that as you grow, you're going to add to the team, and these employees will need to fit into your organization structure in a way that has a positive impact on the business financial success and there is a cost to each position. These overhead expenses need to be included in the financial forecast model. It is important to understand how each position interacts and is interdependent upon each other.

Since it takes <u>people</u> to grow a business, there are three major buckets that we like to look at in terms of the organizational structure. Those buckets are <u>Marketing & Sales</u>, <u>Operations</u> or <u>Production/Service</u>, and <u>Back Office Support</u> (accounting, HR, etc.) More on this in Chapter 3.

Financial Forecasts Case Study:
Commercial Landscape Maintenance & Construction Co.
- Southeastern Region

Overview:

I was contacted by a family-owned landscape construction and maintenance company in the Southeast. They were doing $16 million per year in business. They had worked their way out of a tough financial situation after the recession, but they were still challenged financially with negative profitability and poor cash flow. At the time, the company's owner wrestled daily with the prospect of not having enough cash flow to honor operating cost i.e., fixed and variable costs. He was torn between two strong forces in opposite directions. On one hand, he wanted to invest more in generating new business, on the other hand, he was troubled that this will reduce the company's liquidity and cash at hand for operations cost. He was in a quandary!

They contacted Waters Business Consulting Group in late 2017, and we engaged in the very beginning of 2018. We have been working with them for almost 3 years now. This company has been in existence in the Southeast since 1984, and they are one of the dominant commercial landscape contractors and maintenance companies in the area. The owner has been instrumental in the business growth, and his son has been key to helping them improve their profitability and cash flow utilizing our strategies and their commitment and focus on the numbers.

Process:

When we began our engagement, this commercial construction/ maintenance landscape company had significant debt. Cash flow was very difficult, and this company, while bringing in revenue, was still in negative profit margin. At $16 million, they were running at a negative 5% - 6% net operating income. They should have been able to generate some decent profit to cash flow the business, but there were some costs of goods (labor and materials), pricing, operations, overhead issues that needed to be tightened up in addition to high finance costs.

Financial modeling, using our **Profit by Design Methodology** was key to this company's success. We did an analysis to review their history and understand what got them to this point. One of the key things that stood out is they didn't understand how much revenue was being driven by their different divisions. We needed to separate that revenue from each division, so we could understand the gross profit margins in each division. We looked at each one of those to understand what was driving the margins, and how they were controlling their cost of goods and the margins that were applicable to those divisions. So, once we analyzed that, we did a forecast of what it would take to get them to $18, $20 and $22 million in annual profitability, to improve cash flow, and improve the gross margins.

At the time, although this company was driving top line in terms of the revenue, there wasn't a lot of focus on controlling cost of goods to increase the margin, specifically to control their direct labor and materials costs. They didn't have any purchasing or procurement department in place in order to control purchasing costs by buying materials against an approved budget. They weren't doing proper job costing; they were simply estimating the jobs based on a rudimentary type of an estimating system. Even as an established company of this size, they were taking their costs, then doubling it and adding a certain margin to create an estimate and price for clients. It was clear that they didn't have a very clear pricing strategy which meant they had no control over what their margins were or should be in relation to the labor and materials! Therefore, without an accurate idea of what margin they were using to obtain their price, they had no way of determining if the actual margins were correct. We established that the actual margins were not sufficient to bring profitability and positive cash flow to the business, so we knew that we needed to address their pricing strategy and how they were managing their direct costs.

We spent a lot of time with this client to develop a financial model. We were able to back our way into developing the pricing strategy, and then establish the target gross margins they needed to achieve to ensure profitability as long as revenue targets were achieved and by controlling cost of goods. These steps really helped to improve the operational efficiencies.

One of the other things that the financial modeling did was tell us the kind of revenue this client needed to be driving each month in terms of scheduling production, and then how much they had to have in their pipeline to feed that schedule to hit monthly revenue targets. When we first reviewed their pipeline, there were projects on it but many projects had already been completed, or lost or missing…the pipeline wasn't clean, it hadn't been scrubbed. There was a lot of work to rebuild the pipeline so that we knew we had a solid pipeline of a certain number of bids to fill the schedule to achieve the revenue targets. For example, if the bids in the pipeline total about $10 million, and if they are converting 20% of those to contracts, that's $2 million a month and will get them to approximately $24 million if the bids turn over every 30 days. However, if the bids turn over every 60 days, then they would need to double the pipeline size, and those bids at the right price. That was where the pricing strategy came in.

The financial model is an ideal model for really viewing the results you are trying to obtain. It is a forward look into your financial statement based on trends and assumptions. The actual monthly P&L Statement is a scorecard, but it's historical because it is produced after the month is over. What the financial model does, is it forecasts what we ideally want to get the business to in terms of target revenue, margins, and profitability in order for the company to be healthy. This often becomes the company budget. Then we can measure the actual performance against that forecast, and that scorecard then tells us whether they were successful or not. Our client was not using it as a scorecard. As long as they were driving top line revenue, they believed they were doing okay. Because profitability was an issue, they were factoring all their invoices to facilitate cash flow. Factoring is where you obtain money in advance, based on your invoices, on work in some cases they hadn't even completed.

This is a dangerous cycle that we had to turn around. We developed a pricing strategy and analyzed the history, built a model to target where we wanted to get their business to, and helped them execute. The target was $22 million as our objective by the second year. We determined the gross profit margins that we wanted to achieve, and then identified the revenue targets for each division and the projects and opportunities that would help get us to the

$22 million. We then defined the type of individuals we needed to hire to get there, (because you cannot grow a business without the right people). We looked at what gaps existed in the operations, and this helped us define where there were gaps in the marketing, business development and cash flow. This helped us to have better relationships with their lending partner, in terms of what they were forecasting, and to define the different revenue classes, (or divisions), so we could determine the margins in each of these classes and how we were going to drive the revenue.

Results:

Today, this client has achieved $22 million in annual revenue, improved their gross profit margin to a trend north of 38%. That is up considerably from the 22% - 23% gross profit margin they were at when we began. Today, with higher GPM and a higher net operating income that is up to 9% before finance and factoring cost, this trend will soon eliminate expensive factoring and the finance cost, and they are rapidly paying down their debt. This company has a very clear forecast and budget, and the result is improved margins and cash flow. They understand revenue in each class or division and the margins in those classes, they know where the gaps exist, and they know what revenue they are driving in the months ahead, whereas before they didn't have an idea, they had a very rudimentary idea of what they were going to produce. Now, they know exactly what they are going to produce in revenue each month. For example, they know that in the month of January or February of the coming year, what their revenue will be, even as they sit in the month of October, November or December. So today they have made huge headway, they hit the $22 million, and they hit the increased profit margins. In 2020, the Company will actually trend north of 38% gross profit margin, even though the revenues are down due to the current economic environment. But it looks strong for the second half of the year and for 2021 and their net operating income is up, and as I noted, they are paying down debt. They will be out from underneath their current lending partner by midyear 2021.

The client has seen a huge turnaround, but the key to that was developing a financial model that allowed them to target where they were going. If you don't have a target, then you don't know what you are aiming at. This plan allowed them to do work on the gaps and focus on the areas of driving revenue at the right price and managing the cost of goods and the margins to get there.

Today, they are successful and the son has now been given the reins and promoted to President to run the business! The father realized that finances was not his forte, yet the son had a great aptitude and capacity with these numbers. His father was more visionary, and together the two are a very effective duo in managing the business. We are pleased with the performance of this business as a result of the financial model among other strategies.

Chapter 3
Organizational Modeling

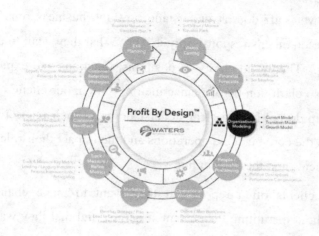

Organizational Modeling is a technique for describing and presenting the functional roles and reporting structure within a business and ensuring that the structure and team supports the goals of the business which is ultimately to provide outstanding service and/or products to customers so that the business prospers. **Organizational Modeling** is used to answer the questions of management and staff about roles and responsibilities as they exist, or will exist, and to develop the structure to achieve the organization's growth objectives while serving the organization's customers.

Organizational Modeling includes:
- Identifying your current operational model.
- Organizational changes - transitional model.

- Developing a growth model by identify key roles required to scale up the business.

In **Organizational Modeling**, the challenges that we hear from our clients are: "My staff doesn't understand how the business runs." "No one knows what each other's responsibility is," or "What they want to do, or what they're doing." There's no clarity of positions, functions and expectations of these roles. No clarity on performance metrics. Often, our client's employees and leadership do not have a clear understanding of their respective roles as they relate to the core business operations and the impact their role has on the customers/clients and the bottom line.

Our clients often report that they want to make changes to the business without disrupting the current structure, and that they want to know what the organization should look like in order to grow to the next level. From there, the conversation often gets deeper. Business owners seek the best ways to scale easier, to hire the right people for the right positions and clearly define their roles.

An example: I recently met with a new client. He had an employee he referred to as "the controller". Yet, when we talked about this "controller's" role and responsibility, it was clear that this title did not accurately describe her position. In this case, the business owner had a great office manager, who provided some operational support. She did manage some AR, but that's a far cry from what a true financial controller would do for any business.

Perhaps you are asking "what is in a title?" and I usually agree. However, in this case, the title made a difference. This employee had a title that did not explain nor match her duties or compensation. Neither she, nor the other staff had a clear understanding of how she fit into the organization. Titles are not perfect, nor the end-all, but they do at least give us some indication of what the different roles and responsibilities are in relation to the overall organization. A great example of specific roles in relation to their purpose, their expectations and expected results are in sports. Each person on a sports team has a title for his or her position and an expectation of performance, as monitored by key metrics. As fans, if we see that a quarterback on a football team, or the pitcher of a baseball team is not performing at a level that is acceptable for that role and position (title), we raise our voices! Just listen to sports talk! We need to have the same commitment and objectives with our business teams.

The key here is that you want to ensure that you have people in the right place, in the right seat and that they're utilizing their strengths, skills and experiences to help manage the business operations and workflow. You won't know that if you haven't defined the positions, and if you haven't defined what or who you need to fill that position to meet the organization's existing needs and future growth needs.

Now, once you get the organizational chart outlined and identify whose roles and responsibilities exist, we are then interested in clarifying each role in detail. We want the specific title, (we will put the names in later) as it relates to the business needs versus a person's name because that person may or may not meet the requirements of the position and title. When there isn't a name put with the title, we know that we are going to fill those positions. We often color code the organization chart so we can see what positions are currently filled and those that are going to be open.

So, once we have the organizational chart outlined, one of the next steps is to define the specific expectations for each of the positions and define this in position descriptions. It is important to be detailed, and outline the responsibilities, the qualifications required, the skillsets needed, the experience and compensation, etc. We can roll this into a position description and an employment agreement as one document or two separate documents. You would be amazed at how many companies don't have a position description or employment agreement for their employees. When this happens, the employees really don't understand what their role is, or the expectations of their position. Then, the business owner wonders why their employees don't perform at their optimum level! However, once the organizational chart is developed and the positions are defined, we begin creating position descriptions for each of the roles, and everything falls into place. These define what the employees are supposed to do to bring value to the business, and the expectations of them in their roles. At this point, we begin to see our client's employees and business thrive because they have clarity on their roles, responsibilities, and expected contributions, value and results to the organization's customers.

We encourage reviewing this document with them on a regular basis. The reason for this is that it ensures that as the organization grows, you are hiring people that are accountable to their roles and responsibilities to help your business meet its goals. If the employees are not fulfilling their responsibilities, they will know it, because you are reviewing their results on a regular basis and providing them feedback. When you review with your employees, they will see that they are providing value and you will be able to acknowledge that as well. This is rewarding for the business, its customers and the employee.

We have some clients who do this very, very well and they meet with the employees weekly to establish where they are at, where they are going, where they need improvements. We have other clients that don't do this as well. When there is no leadership in place for the employee feedback, or guidelines to manage their processes, systems and metrics, that's where the employees have frustrations. Business owners find that their organization is challenged without structure, and we often have to go back to leadership and inform them, "it starts with you". All culture stems from good leadership, which then builds an organization that fulfils its Vision and Mission and engages the employees and ensures that they know they are valued and they bring value to the organization's customers and business. Employees want feedback and a culture that values them. Good leaders do that, and the organization structure allows you to define the responsibilities, align employees with their strengths and the business needs and correct leaders in the organization, and understand each role so that you are utilizing the team's strengths to serve customers and grow the business.

Defining roles is just part of this process. As business owners, we need to identify what we do, and what each role is in the current operational model. Then we must look at what organizational changes need to be made to transition to the growth model, and what that growth model looks like.

Once the new organizational model is done, then we begin to look at the individual people and ensure we have the right people in the jobs for maximum success and we begin assessing the required talent and skills to grow so that we can build out that growth model and begin recruiting those people! Organizational engineering is an ongoing and critical process for any business that is growth minded.

Organizational Modeling Case Study:
Fire & Safety Service and Repair

Overview:

A company that provides fire and safety services and equipment repair has been a client of ours for almost two years. Their focus was to improve the organization in terms of its operations, processes, procedures, efficiencies and to continue to grow, and improve the margins and profitability.

At one point, the owner had considered selling the business as he was frustrated with a lot of their internal processes and the people and he was just worn out. Some of the confusion and frustration resulted from persistent low employee morale and a chaotic culture that undermined collaboration and cooperation between the management and the employees. Internal infighting and rivalry were keeping the owners on edge. Faced with these challenges, leadership worked with the employees at arm's length. Obviously, this did not help the situation. If anything, it made it worse.

Luckily, he came to us. What we have done, is to really help this company define their existing organization structure, and to develop and improve their processes. Through this process, they are now able to understand where their revenue and profit centers are within the organization, and where their dollars were being made in terms of gross margins. This led us to then focus on the organization and processes. One of the services this client provides, is annual inspections that are required by the State to meet fire and safety regulations. In doing these annual inspections, they often find what they call "deficiencies". In this context, a deficiency is where the inspector finds issues with the fire protection system that need to be repaired–and this generates additional work orders and business. This client was generating new business, inspections and deficiencies, but he knew they were losing money due to the inefficiencies across his organization.

The company has done very well since its inception, and the owner has been in the business for over 15 years. He is married and has 2 kids and has a partner that he bought out, in part, due to our joint assessment of the poor performance in the division the partner oversaw. This client also loves to hunt, and to take some time off once in a while, so having a business that functions effectively without him is a priority. However, the organization wasn't allowing the owner to step away to be with family or take that time off to hunt because of the way the team was structured, and he needed to establish accountability, processes, clear expectations and define the profitability of the business. In short, they were not as efficient as they could be, they were lean and cash flow was poor.

With respect to the company's culture, the owner and the team have come a long way. Employee consultation enabled us to gain greater support for our work, thanks to the owner 's permission. This gave us invaluable access to employee support and goodwill that paved the way to a new level of management-employee collaboration. This cooperation has been getting better by the day. The leadership has gone on to create new programs such as Tech Career Track Training Programs, and Educational Programs that coach and support employee growth. Lately, the leader has started taking lunches to his Techs in the field; this is a complete culture turnaround.

Process:

Upon engaging with this company, we focused on helping improve their business cash flow as a priority. We chose to pull the entire team into the process during several meetings, and we worked on process improvement in terms of the DSO, (Days of Sales Outstanding) and improved the Accounts Receivable considerably. The owner said, "If I can improve my cash flow by one week, this would be huge." In his case, this meant from 45 days to get it to about 39 days. With some changes, we helped him achieve 36 days! We improved DSO considerably and the owner is much happier and even let us know that his wife appreciated our effort as well! Our client even said, "my wife loves you guys!"

Since the business owner is happier at work, is enjoying the process and he's been able to take time off to hunt, his general mood has improved at work and at home! Even his employees have noticed a happier, less stressed owner. A side effect of him taking some time to recharge is that it also necessitated us developing the right organization structure. This did mean he had challenges with some of the technicians in the field not being accountable, and as a result, there is a fair amount of turnover of the technicians on the service side and the construction side that we helped him address and resolve. This is common in this type of industry. Through this process, we outlined the organizational structure and determined which employee in each of their respective areas was responsible and accountable to the individual managers. This organizational structure allowed us to have a visual on what the organization looks like today, and then we began filling in where the organization was growing to in the future, and what the team would look like to support the top line/revenue forecast. Along with the future organizational structure, we developed our financial forecast and our financial model. We said, "if your organization is going to get to $9, or $10 million...these are the positions you are going to have to put in place to grow and you are going to have to have key leadership who is accountable and specifically accountable over the different revenue divisions."

In the organizational charts that we develop at **Waters Business Consulting Group**, we prefer to have those specific divisions in an organization chart as revenue divisions to ensure accountability. So, in the case of this client, they have services, and under service there are multiple service areas: Fire Alarm, Sprinkler, Extinguisher, Backflow, and Kitchen Hood Service and Repair. They had a focus on fire alarm repairs and safety inspections and repairing deficiencies, but each of those areas needed focus and to be included in the organizational structure. In addition, they also have a construction division that also does the new installs, which through our analysis, was not profitable consistently. So, as noted earlier, we worked with the owner to close down the construction division and allocated the business resources to growing the service divisions. Although our focus was to outline the organization as it existed at that time, and then what it would look like as they grew and scaled up, this process identifies uses of resources (people) and identifies gaps in the organization.

The key to this, is that you cannot scale a business without *people*...it takes people, strategy, execution and capital. The organizational chart isn't just a picture of who your team is so you can look over it and hang it on a wall. An organizational structure is developed so that you have a clear picture of who the team is and what their roles and responsibilities are to support the business workflow in serving your customers, and to grow the business to the next level. Then you can be in a position to identify where you need additional individuals, where the gaps are in order to get to the next level. I have gone through this process with clients many times and it's amazing how they can see where the gaps and opportunities are for growth if they realign their team and/or hire the right talent. With this client, we are also doing some forecasting on their sales and getting a clear picture on where the sales are coming from so they can look at the type of technicians they need to hire to support their growth.

Results:

In the case of this fire and safety company, they have evolved considerably. We have probably helped revise 15 different organizational charts to get to the current one as a result of identifying gaps and their growth along the way. Because the organization has grown, we had to revise it as it has grown and the newest one is very clear on whose roles and responsibilities exist. The other strategy that was very unique in this situation, was a shift with one of the partners because we shut down a division that the partner was leading and the division wasn't profitable. We had to move this partner into a line role in terms of helping manage technicians and actually working the field as well. So, it was unique in how that came about and showing that on an organizational chart and discussing his role and the changes that would take place. This helped to facilitate the owner's communication in eventually buying out this partner because there wasn't a fit. The organizational chart allows us to have a high-level conversation on the strategies and a deeper conversation on the individuals, their roles, responsibilities and performance and this then allows the organization to identify key performance metrics for objective measurement and accountability, and for the business to function much more efficiently in the case of this client. Today, the owner doesn't want to sell his business, he's excited about growing the top line, improving gross margins and positioning the company eventually for a sale but at a much higher valuation. In short, this owner is smiling on his way to the bank! This case study has demonstrated to us one important lesson; it takes two bangles to make a jingle.

Chapter 4

People/ Leadership Positioning

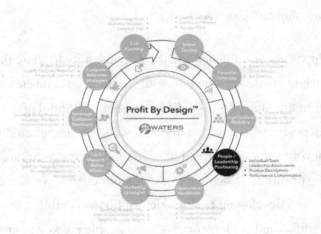

People/Leadership Positioning is the process of determining positions, and personnel in an organization where the responsibility is not just to manage people and processes, but to improve on the system, raise productivity levels, improve staff performance, build a healthy culture and implement the changes to the organization and positions to solidify that improvement for long term growth, stability and profitability.

People/ Leadership Positioning includes:

- Taking 100% ownership & responsibility.
- Acknowledging that successes and failures are a direct result of leadership.
- Leadership assessments.
- Individual assessments.

- Position descriptions.
- Performance compensation.
- Leadership growth.
- Learning through books, audio, seminars and webinars.
- Mentorship and coaching.

Leadership is about influence and the responsibility to share the Vision, the Mission while providing direction with clarity, focus and steadfast commitment. In this step of our **Profit by Design Methodology**, we look at the leadership positions and we determine if we have the right individuals, with the right core values that are in line with the company culture and all key leadership positions. When we work with our clients, we also do get into some refining and developing position descriptions in defining those roles and responsibilities and the key metrics since people are key to growing a business.

You might be saying, well, "I feel like I'm doing everything in the business today," or you might say, "What qualities should I look for in a leader?" or even "How do I provide an assessment of my staff? And then, "What do I do with this information about my leadership team?" Since leaders come with all different backgrounds, we have compiled a list below of some other common issues and questions we hear, but you may have your own too. It is best to be upfront with yourself and recognize where your concerns lie—and then they can be addressed.

Here are some other common questions and comments:

- What should I do with my staff, based on the assessment?

- What do I do with a leader who knows the job really well, but doesn't know how to lead others?
- I can't find good leaders for my business. I have to do everything to make sure things get done right and my employees don't seem to listen or care about the business.
- I don't have time to make sure everyone is doing their job.
- I haven't had a vacation in years.
- Should I pay only a sales commission or pay a flat salary for sales? Or do I pay a draw plus commission?
- Do I develop a tiered commission plan?
- Should I set up a performance incentive program?
- How can I get the most out of my employees?
- When is a good time to promote someone?
- How do I motivate my team and keep them on point?
- When do I know when I need to replace an employee?
- How can I improve my culture and is this important?

This area of the **People and Leadership Positioning** can be one of the biggest areas needing focus for any business, and often we find many business owners are struggling in this area and they may not even know it! Growing your business requires people with the skills, experience and core values that is your culture. Getting great people is always a challenge, especially in a good economic market. But also, some businesses just do not spend enough time developing the people they have. Since great staff is your greatest asset—this is where you really want to focus a great deal of attention.

We work with our clients to develop 100% ownership and responsibility for each position by clarifying roles, responsibilities and helping you set appropriate expectations. Together we make sure that we identify that all success and failure is a direct result of leadership–including yours! Each leader in your organization must understand that their role is about influence and the responsibility to share the vision, the mission and provide direction with clarity, focus and steadfast commitment is on the leader.

One tool we use to grow great leaders, is to utilize **leadership assessments**. Waters Business Consulting Group also does individual assessments, creates position descriptions and develops performance compensation plans. Our team also has to practice what we consult so we do internal assessments, and we continue to invest in our own education and growth to develop as a leader in business consulting, so that we are effective for our clients by reading the right books, and attending seminars, workshops, etc. These assessments allow you to see blind spots, such as vague or conflicting position descriptions or even an employee's misunderstanding of the business Mission and Vision and goals. Ultimately, the position descriptions will include performance compensation tied to key metrics. The metrics come out of the financial data that tells us which numbers we need to drive in order to move the needle specific to improved efficiencies, productivity, revenue, margins, client/customer satisfaction, etc. These metrics provide objective data and focus for leadership. Then, we can grow the leadership team, and leadership growth can be garnered through books, audio seminars, webinars, and leadership coaching of identified leaders.

People and Leadership Positioning is where a lot of business owners struggle because they feel like they are doing everything in the business. Sometimes these owners find it difficult to stop working in their business in order to start working <u>on</u> it.

They struggle with the following questions and concerns:

- What quality should I look for in a leader?
- Am I a good leader?
- Am I developing as a leader?
- I don't have time to take classes or do development.
- I have to do everything to make sure things get done.
- How can I make my employees listen or care about the business?
- I haven't had a vacation in a while.
- I am too overworked and tired.
- Am I accountable to my team or someone else besides me?

These are all signs of poor leadership that needs to change. Leadership is about taking 100% ownership and responsibility. Ultimately, all the success of the organization, the people, the process, the revenue, everything stems from YOUR leadership. So, when I hear business owners blaming their employees or vendors, or the economy or lack of time, I look at them and we have a candid conversation about their own accountability, setting expectations, coaching the team, and having critical conversations with employees. I advise that it's about influence and the responsibility to share the Vision, the Mission and provide direction. In leadership, it's important to first do an assessment so that you understand who you are and to get feedback from your team so that you can make improvements.

A quick example: The owner of the fire and safety service and repair company, said very clearly: *"One of the things I watch with people is their actions over their words."* Now, many of us have heard that before, of course. But to hear the owner say that it is the actions that he monitors, and that he watches to make sure that the actions match the words, is a sign of good leadership.

People/ Leadership Positioning
Client Spotlight:
Aviation Service & Flight Training School

We are working with an aviation company that conducts Pilot Training. What is interesting about this company, is that the owner struggles with some of the individuals that don't perform to the organization's, or owner's expectations. These people consistently don't maintain accountability. The organization's revenues are reasonable, but their margins are poor and not where they could be. After conducting a comprehensive review of the business' historical financial statements, we saw that the net profit of the business was negative in 2019 and was trending in that direction in 2020. In retrospect, it is fitting to say their margins were dangling on a razor-thin edge. If no action was taken, this situation had the potential to implode and impact the survivability of the institution and livelihood of over 32 employees. Above all, its very existence had an impact on the future careers of many pilots. The flight instructors and the business struggled with moving the students through the program in an efficient and effective rate, while generating on-going revenue when students use their hours for classroom, simulation, and flight time. One issue with wide-ranging impact was school's student retention rate. It was down, and the attrition rate was up. Issues surrounding student attrition, retention, and drop-out with refunds compromised investments in labor costs on instructors because advisors were still paid, and this caused significant pressure to the bottom line. Without a doubt, the business needed student retention to sustain profitability and to utilize these funds in helping to reduce business debt. Based on our analysis, this was a critical interdependency issue.

Another unanticipated challenge was classic Air Aviation's billing structure. It was different from the standard processing system in other flight schools. Instead of paying the full cost of tuition up front, students would pay a partial amount at the beginning and then the end of the program. This is a delicate balance between profitability and perishing in debt. You cannot ignore this mid-air suspension. If you do that, you do so at your own peril.

The reason I share this as an example is the owner's approach to leadership. The owner is a great guy, passionate about the aviation industry and his business, and he's also a pilot. He flies for commercial airlines, and he does very well in his profession. For him, it's hard to give up that regular income because his own business wouldn't be able to support him at this time. The business is right on the cusp of breakeven to slight profit. During the economic challenges resulting from the Coronavirus pandemic, they began to see a decline in enrollment and retention of students due to the airline industry demand even though the demand for pilots remains extraordinarily strong. We worked with them through the 2020 pandemic and economic hardship, and we believe that they will survive with our support and strategies, and because there is a huge demand for pilots that has only temporarily slowed but will not diminish for long due to demand post-COVID.

However, here is the challenge. The owner was not present in the office 80% - 90% of each month because he was flying commercial jets. That left no leadership present in the organization. As a result, he got frustrated that his team was floundering and challenged with growth and moving to the next level. At the same time, he hasn't put anyone else in charge and when he did come back in to check on the business, he tried to check in and do the 24-hour leadership and management by assuming that his directives mapped out in a project management software would be followed. Leadership requires a leader to be present and to model expectations and accountability. Leadership takes time because your team needs to know you're invested in them. Not surprisingly, the owner's approach was not effective.

Since he is not flying due to the virus, he began spending more time in the business. We've encouraged and coached this leader to focus on developing the business and developing his people. He acknowledges that he needs to use this time to develop as a leader and he must develop other individuals and hire the right people. We've expressed that if he wants accountability from the employees, he must model it, because all business culture stems from the leader. He needs to hold his employees accountable and coach them up. If they are not coach-able then he has the responsibility to terminate them and find the right individuals. But he first has to develop as a good leader.

While he is not the leader he should be right now, his willingness to engage our services tells us that he has great potential to be the leader he should be...and as a result, he will have a great, and profitable business by design. In essence, his commitment is an abundant demonstration *that the road to success is not painted with wishes, but with brushes and ashes of hard work.*

People/ Leadership Positioning Client Spotlight:
Commercial Mortgage Broker

Another great example: My commercial lender client, Dave, is an outstanding leader. In fact, he says, *"I don't like to manage, but I don't mind leading"* and there is a difference! Leading is influencing people, leading them, and <u>then</u> helping to <u>manage</u> processes and systems. He would rather hire individuals to manage those processes and procedures, (which he is currently working on). He is an outstanding leader in that he has the Vision and influence, as I mentioned earlier, and he shares his Vision and Mission on a regular basis and reviews it with his employees regularly. His entire team lives out the Vision in their work environments.

We continue to work with this owner in developing his leadership skills and he is very coachable and willing to be mentored. In fact, this is one of the characteristics that makes him a great leader–he is willing to evolve! He models what he says he is, and when he says he handles himself with integrity, he does. I have seen him apologize to his employees for simple issues he believed he had mishandled, and this sets the tone of his culture of accountability, integrity, graciousness, and humility. For example, he is able to recognize that small faults in his demeanor may not have been appropriate in a certain situation, and so he holds himself and his team accountable. He's a great leader from the standpoint of establishing the vision and establishing clear expectations. He has mastered the position descriptions with responsibilities and requirements and then specified objectives and clear metrics that the employees need for direction and accountability. He is clear with the employees and the result is that he communicates with the team and manages those expectations on a consistent basis. He consistently trains his staff and even though it's a small organization, he is doing everything right. As a result he is growing, and his fees since I have worked with him have more than doubled. By the end of 2021, the fees will more than triple, (even though he faced serious economic challenges due to the pandemic), and his competitors are struggling to survive in this market. Yet, this client finds a way to be consistent in his leadership and growth.

Above all, I would say that since this owner's core values stand out, he has the respect and loyalty of his team. He is a man of great integrity and cares about helping people. He's vulnerable and open about his purpose and convictions and that's the key to good leadership. He is comfortable in his vulnerability. He can say, "I'm struggling," or "I am afraid," or "I have got this." He has come to understand that he needs to show that he is willing to have the courage to move forward, but also be able to show when he is afraid. Being afraid and having courage are 2 different things. Courage is stepping into those moments when you are afraid and that's what Dave does, and he shares openly so his team and others trust and respect him and model those core values in their culture.

People/ Leadership Positioning Client Spotlight:
Commercial Landscape Maintenance Contractor – AZ

We have a client we've worked with for over 3½ years that is in the commercial landscape maintenance business. He used to play in the NFL, so he understands the value of a team and good leadership and coaching. He understands working together, and he is a great leader from the standpoint of taking ownership and holding people accountable. He also monitors his business metrics and financials very closely and we meet with his team weekly. When we started, we encouraged this client to include his key managers during our weekly sessions given their level of impact on the business. He now includes his leadership team, (the key individuals) in the meetings because they are a part of helping him execute our strategies that's going to help him grow the business. He has grown his business from the time we started working together in late 2016, from $2.7 million to being on pace in 2020 for over $9.5 million. In the 3½ years we have worked together, we have helped him triple his revenue and double his net profit, and he is very focused on growth and monitoring his metrics. But, accomplishing this was achievable because of his leadership and character.

For this company, we are even working on a profit-share program and ownership for some of his key team members. One way to engage team members is to inspire an "owner's mindset" and profit-sharing, in the right organizations, is a powerful motivator.

This owner is a very effective leader because he is transparent, he listens to and includes his key team members, he holds people accountable, he also models accountability, and he is very involved with his business finances. He has a strong vision for the organization, and he is clear on the goals and holding the team accountable. Most importantly, he is open to helping to develop his team, helping each of his team members grow, to be engaged, and find value in what they are doing.

Chapter 5
Operational Workflows

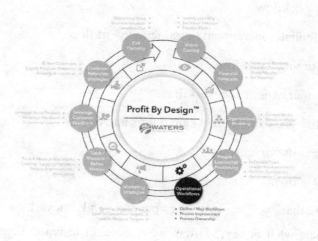

Operational Workflows are the business processes for managing customers and clients, employees and vendors and strategic partners. Operational workflows show how the business runs in a visual format while identifying the key stages of the business processes and procedure and which employees/vendors are responsible for the different stages. **Workflow Process Mapping** is identifying what the organization's specific workflow is that's unique to them and how they deliver or provide the product or service to their customers/clients through the entire process from marketing to sales to accounting to customer service.

Operational Workflows include:

- Define and map business workflow.

- Marketing workflow.

- Sales workflow.

- Fulfillment / operational / production workflow.

- Accounting workflow.

- Customer experience workflow.

- Identify gaps and known pain points and causes.

- Process improvement.

- Process ownership.

Now that you've got the people, and they have clear job responsibilities, what is next? Often, we're brought in with clients who find they are struggling because their business processes are ineffective to grow. Essentially, the processes exist, but they are in the owner's and employee's heads, and not documented, so the team and organizations tend to have ambiguity and inefficiencies in their processes as a result!

All organizations have workflows. Workflow is the process of how a prospect becomes a customer to the point you deliver your product or service, receive payment and then ensure outstanding customer service to retarget the customer and their network again. It starts with marketing and then ultimately sales, and then once you have contracted or engaged, you provide your product or service to the client or customer through an implied or actual contract.

Your workflow may vary depending on if you offer a one-time service, are a retail store, restaurant or a construction company doing remodeling. But whatever the service is, once you have done the marketing and sales, you engage in providing your service/product.

Now, if you are retail or restaurant, the contract occurs when you place your order. There is an understanding that the customer will pay the bill and so you initiate service. But in other businesses, the customer may contract with you, and that contract or agreement is sent to accounting, and then from Accounting they determine the payment terms and the creditworthiness and they then send this to be scheduled to either produce or manufacture, and/or procurement (ordering materials and supplies) and eventually scheduling or coordinating labor and materials to produce the product or service! As you can see, so many factors vary depending on the type of service. Each type of business has a unique workflow, and this requires clarity on the stages and processes and who on your team owns that process.

Even beyond the initial process, there is the actual production, the manufacturing, providing the service, etc. Once that's completed, the back-end usually consists of some form of quality control review with a customer or client, and then there is usually a final payment. And you are still not done! Ideally there is some form of a customer service survey to ensure that you've got an opportunity to retain the customer/client and gain repeat business, and then the cycle continues or restarts.

When the first process ends, it then begins again. We call this **"workflow process"** or a **"client life cycle."** Once you engage the client from a standpoint of marketing, getting their interest all the way to sales through to the delivery of the product or service, and do it well, the client will, (you hope) repeat. All businesses have a client life cycle and have workflow processes. Each one of the businesses can be somewhat different or unique in the details but the high-level processes are the same; marketing, sales, engaging the customer, getting payment, providing the goods and service etc. What we do, is work with the client to map out their specific workflow process because we want to get clarification on the workflow, identify gaps, improve efficiencies and streamline the process so that the workflow process is as efficient as possible by identifying the different workflow stages. We also identify who (employee or vendor) is responsible for that different stage…it could be one or various employees. Then we assign those individuals to the stage that fits their skills and strengths. Once we assign the position (person) responsible, we incorporate this into their Position Description (Job Description), as we noted in our earlier discussion on developing position descriptions from the organization chart.

When we develop these workflow processes, we identify what these steps are from start to finish. We then assign these tasks to key individuals in the organization, because it's people who actually manage the workflow process with the client or customer. Then we establish key metrics to monitor results and establish performance metrics to track leading indicators that tell us what is happening with the client life cycle or flow and how those leading indicators are driving the lagging key metrics (such as sales and cash flow). We identify these leading indicators for marketing, sales, accounting, production/service, all the way through to the end of the process which provides accountability to the employee responsible and brings greater visibility to ownership in managing their business with less stress. This workflow mapping provides us some indication as to where the client or customer is moving through the process, what's happening with the client, are we successful or not successful, etc. In essence, if we are seeing red flags; essentially, are there signs, as leading indicators, saying, *"hey things aren't going well, there are problems."* We flag those as yellow or red. But we also look for the green indicators saying, *"things are going well".* The reason for this is that our goal is to provide for our clients, a high-level dashboard to monitor the workflow and the leading indicators that really drives the business. This helps the owner and key leaders to manage the leading indicators that impact key metrics that influence the business goals often tied to Sales and Revenue, Cost of Goods, Profit Margin, Customer Satisfaction, etc. So, by establishing and managing the workflow process, you move another step closer to ensuring **Profit by Design**. Once this workflow process, or Client Lifecycle, is running smooth, we're able to repeat this over and over by then retargeting customers based on our metrics and the customer's needs.

Here is a personal example: I finally broke down and cleaned my house the other day and I realized; I've done this so many times I have a process that works well. I know where the supplies and tools are. I follow the same pattern each time. I eliminate extra steps and I have created an effective and efficient process.

Any of us who have cooked an egg, or baked cookies follows a process. There are efficient ways to go about doing just about anything. It's the same with a business, even though the processes in business can be different depending on the products or service. However, workflow mapping will help identify your gaps so that you will be more efficient in your business processes.

You may be facing some issues such as:

- Whenever we get a big order, it always seems like we process differently depending on the order.

- Is there always a delay in the marketing department or is there always a delay in the scheduling department.
- We seem to recreate the same information over and over.
- How can we get rid of all the paperwork?
- Anytime there is an order. It's like we're all running around crazy to take care of fulfilling the order.
- I need to improve the way we respond to client orders.
- Should I have one team or five teams?
- How big should each team be?
- One group of people seem to do about 80% of the job. How can I spread the work out?
- How can I eliminate myself from being involved in every one of these conversations?
- What is a workflow map?
- Why would I need one for my business?
- Where do I start?
- There's confusion with my team on who does what.
- The culture of my team sucks.
- I'm constantly finding mistakes and errors of my employees, and I don't have time for training.
- When should I bring on more staff and do I need managers and can I afford them?

These are just some of the pain points that you may have, and one or more of them may sound very familiar to you. In order to make sense of the best business process, we define and map out the business workflow.

Here are some other questions that may be answered by a focused approach to process:

- How do you make sure that the customer experience was done right?
- Is the quality of the good/service the way it needs to be at delivery?
- Do you have outstanding customer service on the back end?
- How do you generate interest and opportunities out there?
- How does it move into sales?
- How is it moved from sales workflow into fulfillment or to the operational workflow in providing the goods or services?
- How do you account for the transaction through your accounting and your operation?
- Do you have a way to track and measure leading and lagging metrics through your workflow?
- Do you have a proactive plan for managing cash flow?

Each of these questions can be answered with a proper business process and are the key areas that all businesses have, but each business has a different process or handles it a little bit differently. Your process may be unique, but all workflows can be improved! After identifying the pain points and causes for those pain points and where the gaps are, we can begin making improvements by walking through the client's workflow map.

An example of operational workflow at work: We just finished going through this workflow mapping process with a commercial HVAC client over about four to six weeks, and we've identified where the gaps are. They have more clarity on their processes after we spent several weeks on just a couple of areas and determined how they handle billing on certain types of services. For this client, we are now moving into refining that process. We then will establish process improvement in order to help clean up these gaps with process ownership, which is assigning individuals on the team and the organization. Once individuals are assigned (and trained if necessary) to own the different phases of the workflow process, they take ownership and then we can look at what metrics we will align with that phase of the process to monitor. Then we can measure how the employee is performing in that phase based on performance metrics and adjust as needed.

An example of monitoring leading indicator metrics: It's not just that you want a salesperson driving $100,000 a month in sales or a million annually. It's the activity that drives sales. You want to look at what kind of activity is driving those sales. The activities based on specific metrics drive those sales numbers based on conversion rates such as; networking, prospecting past or prospective clients, sending e-mails, sending direct mail, building relationships with strategic partners, etc. This is why we start our consulting strategy with financial forecasts. We need to analyze the numbers in order to strategize how to get our clients to their growth goal.

An example or refining the metrics: A construction company that we worked with monitored how many plan redesigns are in the queue as one of its metrics. What we found was that plan design revision requests were a leading indicator of a pending sale. When a designer met with a customer wanting to make improvements on their home and then the customer requested a redesign, closing percentages on design revisions were higher than on new designs. We calculated the number of designs that are in the queue to determine how large the design revision queue needed to be to convert to Sales to fill the production schedule to meet the monthly target revenue.

Because the odds of those closing were much greater, we knew we could establish this <u>activity</u> as a metric. Our goal is to provide greater visibility into how the business is running with greater predictability for the business owner, and this is a big part of our **Profit by Design Methodology,** and we align these leading indicator metrics and performance metrics with the Workflow of the organization and tie them to the individual responsible for that phase of the workflow. This provides our clients with data on how their customers/clients are moving through their process and holds specific individuals on the team accountable to that process so that the business can maximize the efficiencies, revenues and margins.

Operational Workflows Case Study:
Commercial Mortgage Broker

Overview:

My team and I have worked with several clients very effectively to help them develop their workflow processes. I've previously mentioned our commercial lending client, Dave, who is one great example. He needed a large visual way to view his process from start to finish so that he could develop responsibilities, then hire and assign individuals to these processes and eventually use technology to further improve efficiencies.

Process:

Dave wanted to map out his entire workflow process from start to finish when we started in 2018. We literally mapped this out digitally, then we enlarged it on a large format copier and hung it on the wall in Dave's office for weeks. We then further wrote out the details and built each step all the way from the inception of a customer who wanted to borrow money, commercial borrower, to the steps to qualify that borrower, to the steps of gathering the borrower's information and finances to work them through the process with the Loan Processor all the way to the back end of funding and fee payment. We went through each and every stage. This helped to identify, for the owner, where he had gaps and where he should focus his attention, and where he needed to hire support. Then we began to track metrics in all stages to help him establish leading indicators that would provide him greater predictability in where his business was going.

Results:

By tracking metrics, Dave was able to identify where he had inefficiencies and he could make improvements, where they were spending too much time. They were able to identify the types of clients (industries), and the types of loans that were more successful in being funded versus others. They identified the lenders that had higher close rates and more efficient lending processes to reduce funding times. They really analyzed the data and were able to create vast improvements in their workflow process to process more loans with the same staff. This then helped them to create more efficiencies, then we developed the position descriptions for some of the new hires. These new hires have further refined these processes and actually did video recordings and training on the workflow process for future loan processors and other loan associates that will be coming on board. It was very effective to help Dave identify how he was moving a client through the process, and to create greater efficiencies by tracking where they had inefficiencies. Dave now closely monitors their clients through each stage of the workflow along with his team, and he regularly meets with his team on the processes and how to improve. With a clearly defined workflow map along with key metrics, Dave is now scaling up quickly.

Operational Workflows Case Study:
Commercial HVAC Company

Overview:

Another client we worked with recently on the workflow mapping process was Fiat Incorporated, but they really needed help in improving their processes and procedures to create more efficiencies to support their growth.

Process:

As we began to map this out, what we found early on is the team had some discrepancies in how they understood their processes. We often find this with the clients; their misunderstandings or different ideas as to how they are handling key processes in the workflow. For example, with this HVAC client; when a service ticket would come into the organization it would go to dispatch, and dispatch would determine what type of service ticket this was, (urgent, or something that could be scheduled). But there often are other parameters that needed to be identified that were initially being missed.

In mapping out the process, they were able to identify those missing issues, and embed them into the workflow process. This dramatically improved efficiencies, which improved higher close rates, greater productivity, revenue and profits and cash flow. First of all, this provided clarity to the rest of the team; there were a lot of aha moments. But it also proves, because of improved clarity and understanding, there is the obvious issue of less deficiencies because of the understanding, and this also drives out any gaps that are there. One of the other areas pertaining to this client, was with projects. When projects come in they follow a different flow because they are larger and longer in scope; they don't go to dispatch and they need to be sent to the sales team or business development to review the project specification and create an estimate. With that estimate, it then gets communicated to the client to accept before the project is scheduled or coordinated through dispatch to do the scheduling and eventual projects implementation/installation.

Result:

What became clear is that there are different processes that we are able to identify to help clarify what stage it is: a service ticket versus a project. The different rates that they charge for a service vs. a project, and then the rest of it is how they handle the client through the remaining process. We are still working on this workflow with the client, but we have identified several areas of inefficient gaps and we are working to resolve those gaps so that there are greater efficiencies. This process also identifies where there is a need for additional hires. So, with the additional hires we will then be able to use this workflow process to identify what they are responsible for in the workflow and what leading indicators we are going to monitor and the expectations and results we are after with these new hires. These are some of the examples and benefits of workflow mapping. This has greatly helped this

Commercial HVAC client understand their workflow and where they need additional hires and where they need to close the gaps to create more efficiencies.

Operational Workflow Client Spotlight:
Kitchen & Bath Remodeling Company

A past client, who does kitchen and bath remodeling, is another great example. When we walked through this workflow process with them, they said that process was instrumental in helping them to streamline, improve efficiencies, assign responsibilities, track their data as far as results and their progress with all clients. This also helped them build out their project and estimating software application called "Buildertrend".

There are huge benefits of walking through the workflow process as it relates to identifying the customer and client flow and then who is responsible and how we are tracking that client. Then, the process to clean up any of the gaps, as this helps businesses run much more efficiently and profitably by ensuring your employees and vendors are accountable to some phase or stage of the client/customer life cycle in this workflow map so that you move closer to **Profit by Design**.

Chapter 6
Marketing Strategies

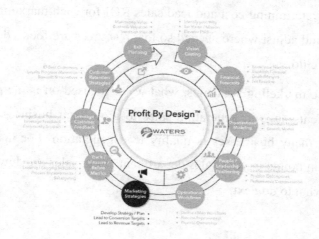

Marketing Strategies are long-term, forward-looking approaches and a roadmap for a business with the ultimate goal of achieving a sustainable competitive advantage by understanding the needs and wants of customers and communicating the solution or needs that the business solves for the customers in order to attract new customers and retain existing ones.

Marketing Strategies include:

- Utilizing the **Profit by Design** strategy, determine the number of leads needed to reach goals based on conversion rates of leads to sales and average sales per lead.
- Developing a **Strategic Marketing by Design Plan** and strategy to generate required leads to meet target revenues.

- Generating awareness, interest and leads into your sales funnel and measure lead to conversions to hit revenue targets.
- Defining action steps and ownership and timeline to monitor and review each marketing strategy.
- Determining cost and lead/sales ROI for each marketing strategy and adjust where needed so that resources are focused on highest return.

In the marketing strategies, what we're focused on is the pain points that most clients have in generating sales to grow their business. The most common for many businesses is quality lead generation. For instance, you may have pain points in your sales department. Your sales are down, and you don't know what to do next.

You may ask/comment:
- I don't know where my customers are coming from, how would I know what new markets to pursue?
- How do I figure out who my ideal customer is?
- What marketing is best for my business?
- I've spent a lot of money on marketing, and I don't know if it was worth it.
- How do I measure the ROI on my marketing spend?
- What is the customer acquisition cost?
- What is a cost per lead?
- Why aren't my leads generating business?
- I've got lots of leads, but what do I do to convert the highest percentage into sales?
- Am I wasting money on leads that maybe aren't converting?

- How do I determine where I should be marketing?
- Should I do Facebook marketing? What about Instagram? What about other social media marketing?
- Should I do print marketing versus online marketing?
- I don't have money to market. What else can I do?
- What is SEO, and should I use it? What about pay-per-click (PPC) marketing?
- How much should I spend on marketing in relation to my entire budget?
- What's the difference between advertising and marketing?

These have been just some of the questions that we've answered with clients. But there are often other questions that clients have and they need help with them. So, we help to put some structure around your marketing strategy, we call it **Marketing by Design**. We utilize the **Profit by Design** strategy to determine the number of leads needed to reach the Sales Revenue goal and that then this approach tells us the kind of opportunities we need to pursue based on those leads. Marketing by Design utilizes proven marketing strategies to interest and influence prospective customers and clients that drive the leads required. Then, we calculate the conversion rate of leads to sales that needs to occur based on your average transaction.

An example: If you're trying to generate $100,000 a month in sales and your average transaction is $10,000 you need 10 of those deals to close. But if your conversion rate is 50%, you need 20 opportunities to meet the goal. If your conversion rate is less than that, you need more leads, or the lead volume needs to be even greater than that.

We help our clients develop a strategic Marketing by Design plan and strategy to generate the required leads. Through this, you will generate awareness and leads into your sales funnel and measure lead-to-conversion to hit the revenue target. You'll implement these tactics, and this helps to define the strategies and define action steps and ownership of each action and a timeline. With this in place, you will be able to monitor and review each of the marketing strategies and make sure that the right people on the team are held accountable to their key performance metrics that are tied to this marketing strategy.

Finally, you will determine the cost of lead to sales and return on investment (ROI) for each marketing strategy and adjust where needed. In essence, we want to make sure that the money is going to the strategies where you're getting the greatest return.

The way that we look at marketing strategies is that marketing is the fuel that drives the engine, and in order to determine the type of fuel that you need and how much you need and how frequently that fuel is injected into the engine, we need to know what RPM this engine needs to run at in order to meet maximum capacity for maximum performance. In this analogy, we may find that we may not need as much fuel as we think we do. Often, I work with clients and business owners, and they think they need to do more marketing to generate more leads. And the fact is, it's not always about lead generation, although that _is_ important. Sometimes, we need to work with their sales team to improve on their conversion rates of leads to closed sales. Sometimes it is in creating higher value such that the customer or client will pay a higher dollar amount per closed transaction.

You can only generate revenue from 3 sources:

- The lead generation.
- How you convert those leads.
- Average dollars per lead or transaction.

In our financial analysis, we determine what the business trends are in terms of financial, operations and marketing performance, and then we establish the financial forecast to determine where the business wants to go and achieve in terms of revenue and margins based on past trends, goals, capacity, marketplace demand, capital, resources, etc. Armed with this information, we are able to project realistic growth in terms of revenues by reviewing marketing data trends.

If a business knows that if they want to grow and they have a 4% conversion rate from lead to close and the average fee is $15,000; and they are trying to generate over $100,000 a month, they know they need almost 7 qualified deals to generate $100,000 in order to achieve their target. This helps them calculate the number of converted leads they need to generate those qualified deals in order to get to their target revenue. At this rate, to get to the $100,000 monthly target, they either need to increase lead flow or conversion rate or average dollars per transaction or combination of all factors. The power is in moving all these factors up so that the liability is not on just one factor. In our example, 7 closed deals at $15,000 each would equal $105,000. At a 4% conversion rate on qualified leads, this would require 175 leads at the 4% conversion rate. Of the 175 leads, they may qualify 20% as opportunities or about 35 qualified leads, but only convert 20% of those leads to actual transactions equaling 7 transactions. What this business needs to generate, will be 175 leads to obtain 20% opportunities and convert 20% to actual transactions or a 4% conversion of leads to closed transactions at 7 qualified customers/clients x $15,000 = $105,000. Based on a $15,000 average fee per deal, they hit their $105K monthly target and achieve **Profit by Design.**

Data Example

Conversion Rate of Lead to Closed:	4%
Average Fee per Transaction:	$15,000
Goal/Month:	$105,000
Qualified Leads to Close Ratio:	7/175
Contacts Req./ Mo to Achieve Target:	700
Contacts Converted to Qualified Leads:	25%
Leads to Opportunities	20%
Leads that Convert to Opportunities	35
Opportunities to Transactions	20%
Leads that Convert to Closed Deals:	4%
Leads that Close per Month:	7

With a marketing strategy, many business owners think it's all about the creative aspect of coming up with a strategy and that drives the lead opportunities, although that's important, the first thing is to understand the metrics so you can develop the right marketing strategy to drive the leads and opportunities. Then you can focus on the creative message to target your specific demographics. What are the number of leads you need to get and in what specific areas do you want to target so that we know how to refine our strategy in terms of the dollars used to generate the leads and the types of target markets we want to go after to generate the leads?

Marketing strategies are more than just developing the creative plan that generates interest to drive leads...it's analyzing the data in order to determine where we want to target our marketing dollars, and what lead generation numbers we need to obtain so that our clients achieve their target revenue numbers. Once we do that, the key is to then track, measure and refine the metrics!

Marketing Strategies Client Spotlight:
Aviation Service & Flight Training School

In another example of an organization improving their marketing strategy, I will share with you the process we went through with the aviation company. We realized that they have a capacity of a certain number of students in their system based on flight instructors, space and staff, but the students have to generate flight hours when moving through their training. When they generate flight hours, our client is able to charge those flight hours to generate revenue. However, if the students don't move through the training track efficiently enough, they are not going to generate revenue for the aviation business. In response, we have established a strategy to help move the students through the training track at a velocity that generates flight hours, that turns dollars that generates the needed revenue to earn a profit and cash flow the business.

We have worked to increase their close rate of new students coming in by developing a unique presentation. The presentation they had before was good. However, we wanted to make it better to increase their closing or conversion rate. While they had an abundance of leads due to demand for airline pilots, they need to do a better job on closing or converting the leads, thereby converting those students to paying dollars. This new presentation helps to convert more students. With more converted students, we are working on a strategy with their flight instructors, the students and the student advisor to ensure that the students are moving through the career track at a steady pace so the flight hours are generated. This is an example of a marketing strategy focused on the presentation based on lead flow from SEO and pay-per-click. Because they were generating a lot of leads, we needed to help them do a better job of closing those leads (students) and ensuring that they generate the revenue as the students successfully pass their flight tests—and now they do!

Marketing Strategies Client Spotlight:
Commercial HVAC Company

Our commercial HVAC client has a focus to grow the business. The commercial HVAC business is seasonal in Arizona, except that there are ways to grow that business by targeting customers for preventative maintenance so that they have recurring revenue every month. We also recognized, in running an analysis on the data, that time and material service drives the project opportunities which drive higher margin revenues. Our focus now in marketing, is to drive towards commercial building managers who need services and preventive maintenance agreements because our analysis shows that out of the services and PMA come the higher dollar projects. The goal is to generate a certain number of contacts in terms of those commercial building relationships that will then generate the time and material (or T/M Services) service work orders that generate the projects.

This strategy also helps to build a stable base of business which increases the overall stability and asset value of the business for an eventual exit.

Marketing Strategies Client Spotlight:
Fire, Water & Mold Restoration Company

We work with a fire, water, mold and asbestos restoration company. They are getting lead activity flow in, but they need the right lead flow in terms of highest margin projects. What we did was analyze the data and determined their highest margin revenue is in fire also and in water. Water drives mold and asbestos opportunities, so we focused on going after those opportunities in the marketplace by targeting insurance adjusters, going after SEO and driving out the opportunities that generate those lead flows. Now they are seeing an increase in higher margin water and mold projects!

Marketing Strategies Client Spotlight:
Commercial Landscape Maintenance & Construction Co. - Southeastern Region

We are currently working with a company that is a commercial maintenance and construction contractor in the southeast. The owners wanted to go from $16 million to $24 million and from minimal and negative profits to consistent profitability and improved cash flow--strong but not unobtainable growth. In order to get them there, we needed to get into the details regarding their financial trends, pricing strategy, estimates that convert to contracts, and analyze labor and materials cost, overhead, finance and factoring and banking fees, etc.

The first step was to track their metrics in terms of leads, estimates, verbal approvals, contracts, etc. We looked at their pipeline and the ability for it to feed a schedule to produce $2,000,000 per month in work to achieve $24M annually. This meant that they were going to have to do somewhere in the neighborhood of a little over $2 million dollars a month. Based on that, they need to be able to convert $2 million dollars a month from the pipeline of opportunities to fill the schedule 30, 60 and 90 days out. So, to push the schedule out 90 days, that is about $6 million that they need converting from the pipeline of contracts that converted from estimates to feed the schedule. To convert $6 million, and if they are running it at 20% conversion from estimate to contracts, they would need $30 million that has to be in the pipeline to convert $6 million in order to ensure they fill the schedule 90 days forward. Then we figured out how many bids they need to prepare and to submit to get to $30 million to convert that $6 million. Since they need $30 million approved and going to contract in the pipeline, they may have to talk to, and prepare estimates/bids for $100 million worth of opportunities based on converting 30% of the estimates to contracts.

How do they get to $100 million opportunities? This means they have to touch and contact a certain number of people to see those opportunities develop into a qualified opportunity that eventually generates a proposal or a bid that eventually gets into the pipeline, and the pipeline converts to $30 million in contracts, those contracts convert to $2 million a month or $6 million at 90 days out. That's the flow and partial equation to **Profit by Design**. Having all those details, we are able to look systematically and strategically on how we then develop the marketing strategy to fill the pipeline with opportunities.

Chapter 7
Track/Measure/Refine Metrics

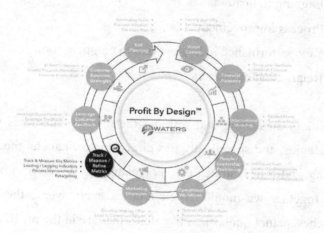

Metrics are measures of quantitative assessment used for comparing and tracking performance and results. Tracking, measuring and refining metrics is critical for running an effective, efficient and profitable business. Metrics integrates with all our methodologies, and specifically ties directly into financial modeling and Marketing and Sales Strategies and can also flow into customer service, quality, core values, leadership, etc. Metrics are objective data, and if tracked consistently, this data will tell you vital information about your business trends. Once you have a pulse on your data trends, these metrics will provide insight on the past performance and the future direction your business is going. This essentially provides you greater predictability and time for planning and making good decisions with less stress.

Examples of metrics to track/measure/refine include:

- Track and measure key metrics.
- Leading indicators.
- Lagging indicators.
- Process improvement.
- Key performance indicators tied to compensation
- Retargeting customers.

Tracking, measuring and refining the metrics integrates with all of our methodologies, and specifically ties directly into financial modelling and the Marketing and Sales Strategies. For example: We have a commercial lender, and together we monitor their metrics every week; the number of ticklers, touches, actual quotes and live deals that are in the pipeline based on the activity. He has a goal of 100 touches a week for each of his sales staff each week. That turns into what he calls "ticklers." Touches are no different than contacting a qualified opportunity. That's the leading indicator. Those numbers tell us very clearly their trends towards actual deals based on historic conversion rates, and these metrics expose where the focus needs to be put to close gaps. So, to ensure you're tracking the right metrics, we help our clients determine what to measure, then how to track and measure key metrics–just as in this example.

We also have used the data to look at where they had the highest percentage of closes in terms of lenders and the types of loans, and which loans close faster. We then use this data in our marketing strategy to identify lenders that are making loans on those types of commercial opportunities, and then we market to find those types of borrowers out in the marketplace. By tracking and measuring and refining the metrics, we use that data to refine our marketing strategies to increase efficiencies and productivity in the workplace. We also use these metrics in monitoring operations…not just marketing but operations such as managing our cost of goods and our overhead costs, our operational work flow, quality, customer service, etc.

One of my commercial landscape maintenance clients monitors weekly average hourly pay rates against target hourly rates along with average hours used compared with budgeted hours allotted by property, by crew and by Account Manager. This data allows our client to control his labor cost and ensure maximum productivity of the crews each month. These are some of the many areas of business operations we track, measure and use the data to measure our client's performance to their advantage. Another client monitors Technician's total hours scheduled against their standard 40-hour work week to ensure they maximize the Tech's productivity and billable hourly rates. This ensures they leverage their resources to achieve maximum revenues and profits.

The beauty about metrics is that they are what they are, they are objective, and they are factual and will tell you a story of past or trending performance. Yet, many clients do not understand how to use this hard data.

Our clients often ask:

- What are the key metrics?
- How do I begin to track the metrics? Can we track those metrics?
- Why are key metrics important for my business?
- How do I establish leading metrics in order to proactively manage my business?
- I'm tracking reporting, but I do not know what to do with the data once I get it.
- What do I do if my key metrics are too low or too high?
- How do I use key performance metrics to incentivize my team?

We help create the Leading Indicators and then the Lagging Indicators. For example, getting a financial report to tell you what your profitability was, is a lagging indicator. We want to develop leading indicators that impact or have influence on that lagging indicator of production, revenue and profitability. Then we look at process improvements, where we can affect change on the entire process with both the team and the workflow that each team member is responsible for in the workflow process.

By tracking and measuring and refining the metrics, we use that data to refine our marketing strategies to increase efficiencies and productivity in the workplace. We also use these metrics in monitoring operations, not just marketing but operations such as managing our cost of goods and our overhead costs. So, these are some of the many areas of business operations we track, measure and use the data to measure our client's performance to their advantage. And those are key areas to look at in your own business to establish some key metrics and measurements that you can track and discuss with your team to increase accountability, focus, production and ultimately **Profit by Design**.

Marketing Strategies Client Spotlight:
Fire and Safety Service & Repair

Our fire and safety company client generally knows what they could generate in annual inspections revenues. These annual inspections are mandated by State and Federal law. Out of those annual inspections, a certain percentage of those generate a certain amount of what they call "deficiencies"; that means additional service repair work based on a broken system, fire alarms, extinguisher, back flow, sprinkler system etc. In analyzing the data, we know what they have trended, in terms of annual inspections over the last several years, and what their ratio of annual inspections is in relation to deficiencies.

So now we are tracking what their annual inspections are in terms of revenue to forecast for future month's revenues, and how many deficiencies they drive based on annual inspections. This tells us the kind of support they need in terms of service techs, and this also tells us the gap between that revenue of annual inspections and deficiencies and the additional service repair work they need to obtain to get to their target revenue number per month and per year.

For example, they are doing $150,000 a month in annual inspections. They generally are generating another $100,000 - $150,000 in deficiencies per month, let's call that $300,000 per month for annual inspections and deficiencies. But they want to get to $500,000 per month. So that's a

$200,000 gap in terms of additional service repair over and above annual inspections and deficiencies each month that they need to obtain to achieve their monthly target revenue.

Then, we ask; *"What type of clientele do we pursue to obtain and schedule the added service and repair work to get the other transactions to generate $200,000 per month?"* This requires our client to go after other opportunities in the marketplace and establish strategies to challenge their sales team. If they have a 50% close rate, they need to generate $400,000 in proposals or estimates to close 50% to get the other $200,000 per month, but we have realized the cycle time takes 45 - 60 days. Based on the math, that requires our client to generate about $600,000 to $800,000 in proposals to actually close $200,000 a month in order for these deals to cycle into the schedule. With this objective data, we can build a strategy and metrics to achieve these target numbers.

Now the marketing strategies; where do we get the $800,000 in opportunities? We have to find those markets or customers and we target those markets in the marketing strategy to generate the leads. In this case, direct sales with the sales force, strategic partners and we also do SEO and paid per click advertising, Google advertising. In essence, we did reverse engineering. Metaphorically speaking, we figured *"how many guests and dignitaries will attend a wedding"* and we worked backward in finding a location, budget, suitable time, and a befitting facility for safety, and availability of parking.

These are simply examples of the metrics combined with marketing, and shows how the tracking, measuring and refining is so integral to the step of marketing strategies. Out of the marketing strategies comes the need to track and measure and refine the metrics!

One of the many reasons our team of consultants has enjoyed working with this client is the willingness to be learn and be coachable. Our involvement has largely been a smooth process; however, it took us a lot more commitment to get employees to fully embrace accountability as a critical metric in measuring individual and team performance. Our diagnostic approach relied on the use of data based on the good old "marketing mix" model. Beyond the traditional model, we emphasized the use of Web *2.0* tools technologies in marketing. This approach leverages elements of the traditional model (product, price, promotion, and placement); as well as web 2.0 marketing tools such as Google clicks, Facebook ads, and LinkedIn marketing. For obvious reasons, this shift did put the spotlight on sales staff because these tools lend themselves to greater analytical scrutiny. As expected, this met with some steep resistance, neglect, frustrations, and neglect on the part of some of the parties involved. In the long term, the client has come a long way in this process, and we are proud of the slow but necessary transition to increasing profitability, one analytical metric at a time.

Track/Measure/Refine Metrics Case Study:
Fire, Water & Mold Restoration Company

Overview:

In recent months, we started working with a restoration company. The owner wants to scale the business to a new level by growing top line. We needed to build a solid and strategic plan to accomplish this. This client is struggling to retain its technicians and letting technicians know that the company is not looking at just their performance but rewarding them for doing good work as well. The company also wants to generate more Google reviews from customers to increase business and visibility on social media platforms.

Process:

We developed the tracking program to address this concern. The objective involved us creating incentives for the technicians and their teams that were performing well. To do this, quality technicians need to be recruited, trained, and retained. A comprehensive recruiting, training, and retention program is essential. Once technicians are on board, we establish key performance metrics that gauge their performance and not only incentivize them to achieve what the owner wants them to achieve, but to have them focus on certain areas of responsibility with a newfound sense of accountability.

In this case, the restoration company does asbestos, water, fire, and other disaster mitigations. When they go in to do a cleanup, it is important that the technicians share with the client their goal of receiving a five-star review. We instructed them to share this goal with the client, and that they will focus on key areas of performance while on the job. When the customer measures their performance afterward, we want them to measure their satisfaction against those areas. We created a simple scorecard that the technicians hand to the customer after completion of the job, which explains these performance areas and includes a QR code on the back that links the customer to a Yelp or Google or other review so that the customer can easily rate the technician and the business performance.

Results:

We essentially decided how we are going to attract and measure technician performance, and then incentivize them to shoot for five-star performance. This plays into a strategy we call "what gets measured gets done." In order to ensure the technicians perform at a high level and get five-star reviews for the company, we have to measure and report their performance regularly. We do this by focusing on key performance areas and delivering bonuses for meeting these targets and present this on an internal dashboard for all employees to view.

If technicians get five-star reviews, they get $100. If they get four-star reviews, they get $60. If they get three-star reviews, they get $40. If they are below this, they lose the bonus amount and fail to build up the pool. At the end of the month, the pool is allocated and gets paid out to technicians who were part of the success. This is tracked per job and per technician on that job, with additional consideration of whether they got five, four, or three stars. Each month, an individual could earn several hundred dollars or just a few. Over the course of a month, assuming the company is doing 15-20 projects, the bonus pool adds up to $1,500 – $2,000 in bonuses available to share with anyone who was instrumental in the success of those projects and the favorable reviews.

The tracking of this information, per job and individual, is displayed publicly throughout each week and month so there is peer accountability. It is maintained in real-time using what we call "real performance accountability."

This ensures all technicians perform. No one wants to not perform and be the weak link. If they do, they shouldn't be on the team.

Today, the technicians are happier because they feel rewarded and recognized, the business is happier because the technicians and teams are focused on doing quality work, and the owner is happier because he is receiving quality reviews that drive new business while retaining quality technicians and employees. This is how the *tracking, measuring, and refining* of performance is done for the restoration company. In this case, the long-term goal is to create additional incentives and generate more revenue and referrals with five-star reviews. Another step towards **Profit by Design**.

Track/Measure/Refine Metrics Case Study:

Carpet & *Flooring Company*

Overview:

A flooring company was challenged with getting too many "hot sheets," or reports showing they were not performing to the high standard they needed to perform at with their customers for floor installations. There were challenges in the process, including the communication and final delivery of the product or service, which left customers unhappy.

It cost money for the company to go back and resolve issues, leading to fewer Google reviews or low ratings. A measure was developed to track, measure, and refine performance metrics to see that the installers were incentivized to do high-quality work, leading to less hot sheets, more money, greater efficiency, and happier customers that are willing to provide five-star Google reviews which brings in more customer opportunities.

Process:

The sales team was having a similar problem. The sales team did a good job of tracking their activity and conversion rates and average dollars per transaction, but they needed to be motivated to drive higher average dollars per transaction, higher gross margins, and higher conversion rates. We focused specifically on those areas, so there was visibility in how they were performing. Although that is carried out in the company's weekly Monday morning meetings, these meetings were only going over the basic sales routine. It was suggested that the team report their metrics and openly share what they are doing to drive new lead opportunities at each meeting instead. This increased both activity and accountability, leading to higher sales and revenues.

Results:

We developed performance incentives for this same company that does carpet, vinyl, and tile flooring. With five years in business, today, they are performing at a higher level than when we last worked with them 3 years earlier. Nonetheless, they want to create higher efficiencies within the organization in terms of sales, conversion rates, margins, and performance. To do this, these four areas must be tracked.

1. Determine where (what activity or key data) they want to track performance.

2. Determine how they are going to track the key metrics.

3. Define how they are going to incentivize and display what they are tracking for peer accountability.

4. Update performance metrics regularly or the data will be meaningless, (like tuning into a ball game and not seeing an updated scoreboard).

For the sales team, we are going to measure top-line sales and how they sell over and above their current trend (i.e., revenue on a monthly basis), what their average sales are per salesperson, per month, what their average conversion rates are per salesperson and on average (i.e., how do they convert from a lead to an actual sale), what their average gross margins are, and how they are driving gross margins.

For the installation team, we are going to focus on being on time and presenting to the customer, and tracking how the job process went, the quality of the job, and whether or not the team got a five-star review for the installation process from start to finish, including quality of install.

As mentioned, each metric will be tracked. Similar to the restoration company, installers will communicate that they are looking for a five-star review and identify the areas they want to be measured by the customer. If they perform to a five-star standard in each area, they will ask for a five-star review at the end of the job. By handling it this way, it is much easier to ask the customer and receive a five-star review from a happy customer and this provides accountability to the installers.

The benefit of measuring performance in these areas includes increased efficiencies, increased referrals, increased sales, more satisfied customers, and higher revenues, margins, and profitability. Overall, the ROI is huge.

We mentioned the principle of "what gets measured gets done." Meaning, once you begin tracking and measuring performance and results with consistency, and when people realize they are being measured by their performance, they will do the necessary activities required to influence the outcome so that when reviewed, they are recognized as either competent or not. Another statement that resonates with companies like this one is "what is expected must get inspected." Here, the beauty about tracking is it shows you are inspecting the expectations of your sales and installation teams. We created a display board that lists performance metrics for the teams, where each get added incentives and bonuses for meeting/exceeding targets. Public posting of this data drives the human behavior element of performance and increases activity and results, generating higher revenues, margins, close rates, and profitability and improved cash flow.

Track/Measure/Refine Metrics Case Study:
Radio and TV *Media Buy Company*

Overview:

We have been working with a Media Buy company which purchases media time for businesses, specifically ministries on the air, television, and radio. This client has done a great job growing the business over nearly 20 years, but the owner admits to not keeping his team accountable. Before engaging with this client, we spent time analyzing their data to understand trends in terms of revenue, conversion rates, and average transactions to understand where we need to go to drive top-line performance, conversion rates, and target opportunities. Once metrics were fully identified, we could figure out how to track them and incentivize and display that data to motivate the teams.

Although the company saw increased sales over the last 15-20 years, it was clear it was not performing at the level it could be performing. The team was not being held fully accountable. There were no target sales numbers. The actual metrics to monitor, both in terms of results and activities associated with it, were missing.

As the project progressed, our team of consultants felt that the company was trapped in a time-and-space capsule with poor internal visibility on what it needed to confront swiftly. On one front, the company was over-depending on the owner's contribution to sales, on the second front, the company needed to develop new sustainable revenue channels given the gradual decline in the significance of the traditional advertising media like Tv and radio. The third and focal front of contention was employee role and contribution. Analytically, the employee 's contribution was ambivalent. If the employee quit suddenly, that would be a risky to replace the 25% in driving sales. On the other hand, the employee's contribution was less than desirable. It raised questions such on the role of training and coaching the employee to increase production to a level that enables the owner to spend more time on mid-t long term strategic business development.

Process:

We developed the analysis to measure their trends and establish goals and leading indicators to monitor performance. Here, the challenge was that the current salesperson was driving less than 25% of total business sales, while the owner was driving over 75%. The issue was to bring this split closer to a 50/50 or 40/60 split. If the salesperson could not meet this, the question then became whether the person should be on the team at all or replaced with someone else.

A process to create accountability and coaching opportunities was developed. This ultimately will grow the business, increase the asset value, minimized pressure and stress off the business owner, balanced out the sales portfolio of clients, and improved top-line revenue and gross margins.

Results:

We have weekly cadence meetings where these leading indicators (activity-based metrics) and results are reviewed to make sure teams are on track. The goal is finding key performance metrics that can be measured and establishing certain activities that drive them. Here, once we have analyzed and determined the business's current trend, we could establish a target goal. Currently, they are trending at about $12 million annually. If they want to get to $20 million, for example, we will look at what it takes to get there by identifying key metrics in terms of activities, daily contacts, conversions, and sales. Conversion rates and average transaction rates will be most important here, and so we must know how they translate into sales in the short and long-term.

Once we track all this, it will again be displayed publicly for everyone to see and review. Those performing at the target will earn their incentive. For the business, this will increase sales over time. In this case, 75% of sales are driven by the owner alone, but he wants to offset that so he's only 30% - 40% of the sales and the rest is driven by the remaining team. Tracking will allow us to see how the trend is taking place so we can justify why we are holding the team accountable and recruiting, hiring, training, and developing other salespeople to augment. Furthermore, it explains why we might bring in new digital and online marketing strategies and add these to traditional services, which are standard media buys. These new services will grow the top-line revenue and stabilize the business to lessen the owner's involvement with sales and to balance out sales revenue.

Long-term, this shift will increase the asset value of the business so it can be sold for much more than if he was still selling 75%. The goal is to grow the business to $30 million, with the owner doing only 30% of the sales with higher margins and conversion rates, and a more balanced revenue stream in terms of the salespersons managing it and new value-added services for clients.

In Conclusion: These examples show how metrics can be tracked, measured, and refined. They are used to inspect what is expected and identify what needs to get done. By doing this, we identify gaps and make corrections through coaching and accountability to ensure we are moving toward **Profit by Design**, not profit by accident.

Chapter 8
Leverage Customer Feedback

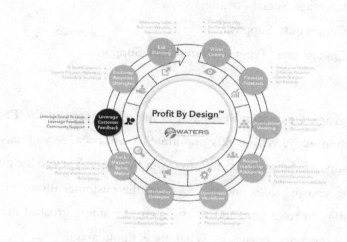

Customer feedback is the reviews, the testimonials, or the suggestions that your customers give you after purchasing a product or services. This feedback can be leveraged to indicate to prospects that your business is worthy of consideration. In today's online business environment, we have found that many of our clients see a measurable increase in opportunities that are directly tied to customer reviews, client testimonials and positive customer scores. We encourage all businesses to build a consistent process to ensure an outstanding customer experience so that you can confidently ask for positive customer reviews that will notably impact your sales and long-term stability of your business.

Ways to improve social standing:

- Leverage Customer Feedback.
- Leverage Social Position.
- Community Support.
- Engage your Team in Community Support.

Leverage Customer Feedback is the eighth area in the **Profit by Design Methodology**. Why is this important? Well, because your customers are the ones that are helping you to grow your business! They're the ones that are providing you the sales and the revenue, the customer ultimately is the one that's going to refer you, and referrals are the single greatest marketing strategy to grow your business! What they think about your product or service is arguably the most important part of the equation.

Some owners still tell/ask us:

- If I am selling, why do I need the customer feedback?
- How do I leverage the comments we get from customers?
- Should I be using my personal profiles or a business profile?
- My customers always tell us they like our service, but I don't know how to ask them to review us.
- We've had some negative feedback on social media, what do I do?

There are many other pain points too, and nowadays, more people are aware of feedback, because of reviews on Google and Yelp. In the past, if you were a Member in Good Standing with the Better Business Bureau, that was sufficient. Today, it's all about the reviews online. So, you must focus on how you're using that to your advantage, both in terms of working with your current customers and getting their positive feedback. In the rare case that you may get any negative feedback published online, you must address it immediately and well. There are techniques to respond to the customer reviews that are not favorable, and those that are prudent to turn those situations around. The power of online reviews can't be understated. A lot of new opportunities are born out of the online reviews. So, we help you leverage customer feedback.

In order to leverage your social position and the community support in getting good customer feedback, we will help you establish a Customer Feedback Program. You often find your own employees, for instance, are a good place to start. You can incentivize the technicians, for example, to ask for feedback from the customers by posting Google reviews. It is even possible to calculate the volume of business you have, and the minimum number of Google reviews you should have each month based on that volume. Any reviews (Google and others) over and above that base amount or trend, and you can provide a bonus to employees who help obtain these reviews as an incentive. Our objective is to tie as many employees as possible into the same Vision/Mission and Commitment as the owner regarding Sales, Controlling Cost, Improving Margins, Quality, Customer Service, Profits and Cash Flow AND Customer Reviews, etc. These are all areas to incentivize your employees.

Customer Feedback of any sort is critical for us as individuals to grow, and it's just as important for your organization because it provides you with an outside perspective that is more objective and not biased based. I would encourage you to find any way possible to get feedback from your clients or customers, and there are various ways that you can go about that. We have outlined some of those in this chapter. One of those ways, is through reviews and surveys and asking for feedback. You can meet with your clients individually, or in person depending on the type of business that you have. For professional services, it is fairly easy to ask a customer if they will allow you to take 15 minutes to ask you some questions about the services provided. And then it is very important that you take notes! You can also ask clients to fill out a survey using an online experience via a receipt, or, possibly best of all, to ask them to fill out a Google review.

Any form of survey where you are providing customers an opportunity to provide unbiased feedback and input on their experience is valuable. You should solicit feedback on why they chose you, why they remain doing business with you, the quality of service or product received, and ultimately the value they received. And as much as we all want glowing reviews, you want realistic feedback too! Even feedback that potentially offends you can be relevant. You want constructive and very candid feedback, because that's what's going to offer you the opportunity to make real improvements to meet the real demand of the customer in the marketplace.

Now, just one customer feedback about your product or service is not sufficient. You need to get feedback from various customers across the board, because that's going to give you a good sample size. Again, one of the best forms of feedback that really helps to drive new revenue opportunities are Google Reviews and Yelp Reviews because other customers or clients see these reviews and they realize that if those customers were happy, then the likelihood that they will be happy is also good. Reviews provide confidence and credibility to existing and new customers.

An additional value of reviews is that it also tells your customers or clients that you care, and you value their feedback. Often when I request feedback/reviews, I have let my clients or customers know, I value their input so I would like to ask for their opinion; then you ask the question. You can do this in terms of a physical survey questionnaire or an online form, or you can hire an organization that will actually do this service for you. But remember to be very thoughtful and intentional about the types of questions you are asking, so that you obtain the constructive feedback that will help you to make improvements across all sectors in your business, from Marketing, Sales, Operations and Delivery of the product and service. Remember, the goal is to create "Raving Fans" (If you haven't read Ken Blanchard and Sheldon Bowles book, "Raving Fans", it is worth the read). Another great tip is to ask for feedback from your employees! The team also has great ideas and very real ways to improve or grow your products or services.

Leverage Customer Feedback Client Spotlight:
Commercial Mortgage Broker

One of the examples I have is a commercial lender and I have mentioned this client in a few other chapters because the owner does such a good job of tracking metrics and being open and transparent to growth, (which is a sign of a good leader ... someone who wants feedback). Internally, he provides feedback to his team so he models what he wants his team to do with his customers. So, for his team to get bonuses, they have to get feedback from the customers that provide them insight into how they are performing and how the delivery of their services went from the customer's perspective. He utilizes this to make improvements, and he also utilizes this to pay bonuses to his employees. He does this through a questionnaire at the very end when the loan is complete and funded. This is required for the Loan Processor to obtain a bonus. They are heavily incentivized to get the customer feedback from the customer or client in this case.

Leverage Customer Feedback Client Spotlight:
Kitchen & Bathroom Remodeling Company

Another example is with a kitchen and bathroom modeling company. They expressed in the very beginning their goal was to provide a 5-star service each and every time. Yet, this client was not seeing any Google Reviews to back up their promise. We wanted to increase the number of referrals as well as reviews to drive more leads and more opportunities. In order to do this, we outlined a presentation explaining to the customer that when they started on the project, the goal was to provide the customer with a 5-star experience through the entire process. If at any point if the customer felt that the remodeling team were not delivering a 5-star service all the way to the completion of the remodeling project, all the customer had to do was say so and corrections would be made along the way. And this is because, at the end of the project, they are going to ask for a 5-star review from the customer. The company is trusting that they would have delivered that 5-star service to earn the stellar review. Before the service begins, they outline and present the key points that the customer will grade on the company's performance.

Here is an example of review/survey questions:

- How was your experience in contacting our organization? In this case, with this remodeling company?
- What was the experience like in terms of getting a proposal or quote, and did we listen to your needs and provide you with a competitive bid?
- Grade us on a scale of 1 - 5, with 5-star being the best, were we on time and efficient during the remodel process.
- Did we leave your property clean in between the times we started and stopped on your project?
- Was our work done with quality and did we meet or exceed your expectations?

Of course, there are many other types of questions, but this gives you an idea. The final question we use, and I recommend for most clients, is: Are you so satisfied with the completion of your project (or service) and the quality of the project such that you would refer us to family or friends?

These are examples of feedback to solicit. This is what the remodeling company has implemented, <u>but that is just the first step</u>. Next, it is important that they have internal meetings to look at how to make improvements in the business based on this critique from customers.

Leverage Customer Feedback Client Spotlight:
Commercial & Residential Janitorial Company

Finally, here is an example with a commercial and residential cleaning company that does residential home cleaning and commercial office cleaning. We worked with them in setting up a customer review program with their crews where the crews would get feedback from the customer on the timeliness, the quality and the efficiency and we graded the crews based on whether or not a customer had to call to say they didn't complete the work or may have missed something. Bonuses would be paid based on these criteria and based on referrals that the customer would send to the business and based on Google Reviews. The crews received a bonus based on how satisfied the customer was and if the customer didn't call back and complain that something was missed. Bonus was also paid when a customer referred them or posted a positive Google Review.

These examples show different strategies of how to solicit and use customer feedback to improve processes and procedures, efficiencies, quality, margins and customer service and you can do the same for your business to reach your **Profit by Design**.

Chapter 9
Retention Strategies

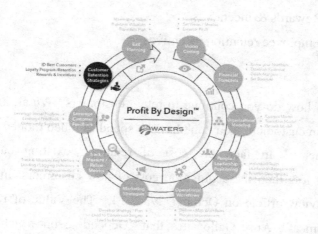

Retention Strategies refer to policies and systems which companies follow in order to retain customers and reduce the need to continuously find new clients. The main goal is to meet and exceed the expectations of customers, create loyalty, and improve perception of the company based on the customer's positive experience, without losing sight of the company's goals to ensure maximum return on investment. An important strategy to client retention is employee retention so this must be incorporated into the plan since your employees are a key extension of your business and the service or product you provide to customers.

Some examples of Retention Strategies:

- Identify best customers.
- Delivering outstanding products and/or services
- Loyalty program.
- Retention program.
- Rewards & incentives.
- Employee retention incentives

Now how do you continue to retain customers? We all know that if you can retain customers, you don't have to spend as much money going after new customers! In fact, the cost of retaining existing customers is considerably less than the acquisition cost of new customers. In a Harvard Business Review article on October 29, 2014, "The Value of Keeping the Right Customers", Amy Gallo sites that "Depending on which study you believe, and what industry you're in, acquiring a new customer is anywhere from five to 25 times more expensive than retaining an existing one." This is based on research by Frederick Reichheld of Bain & Company (inventor of the net promoter score), stated; "research shows that increasing customer retention rates by 5% increases profits by 25% to 95%."

Here are some of the common pain points:

- I do not know what a best customer is. Is it by the amount they purchase? Is it by how nice they are, how loyal or frequent they purchase?

- What is a loyalty program or retention program? How does that work?

- I can't figure out how to attract customers and what they spend.

- What kind of loyalty program is best for my business?

- How does it help if I discount my product or service (seems like I just make less money)?

So many times, the business owners we work with will tell us they do not know who a good customer will be, or how to retain them. So, we want to profile that ideal customer so that we target them in our marketing. We can review our customer data trends to help determine who is buying our products and services so that we can develop unique retention strategies. There are many types of customer retention strategies that help you maintain great clients and drive referrals from your customers as well. In this phase of the process, we help you to identify your best type of customers, and your ideal customer profile so that you can target and develop loyalty programs so customers will repeat and repeat more often.

Over the years, we have turned the customer feedback process into an artform that we deploy to help our clients make informed decisions to boost the bottom line. Without feedback that is emotionally deep and intellectually rich in terms of likes, dislikes, fears, concern, frustrations, nightmares, and exasperations that clients express, it is not possible to determine what services or products are suitable. Without information is both qualitative and quantitative, you how do you know what kind of adjustments to make? You risk making a costly investment in a system that has no value to the customer. For this reason, WBCG spends a significant amount of time learning about the client's tastes and preferences. When this is done right, it enables our clients to perform to the clients 's expectations, or as some people put it colloquially, *"he who pays the piper dictates the tone"*.

Depending on the types of product or service you offer, you may be thinking, "My customers only buy once, so this doesn't apply to me." If you are a remodeling company, for example, it is possible that a client may only use your service once, or once every 6-10 years. But that does not mean you cannot leverage this relationship with a referral program. A referral program could encourage these customers to provide you with new leads, you could partially fund the client to promote an open house to showcase their home improvement, or a testimonial program could motivate more prospects or neighbors to convert. For returning customer opportunities, a retention program is key, especially if you're in retail, hospitality, restaurants or a service, or any business where they use a service regularly.

Remember, a **Customer Retention Strategy** is in addition to the points that we have made in this chapter about other ways to improve customer retention. The Customer Retention Strategies are a thoughtful and deliberated strategy because the amount of dollars that you spend per customer to acquire said customer is expensive. If you don't know what your customer acquisition cost is, I would recommend you look at acquisition cost in terms of how much marketing, plus how much you spend on your team to market and to close a contract or provide a service with a customer or client. Whether you are in the restaurant business, or you are a dentist, or you are selling consulting, you incur a cost to acquire customers. For example, if you are a remodeling business or manufacturing business or auto repair business, there is a cost to acquire each customer. You will want to look at those costs and figure out what your conversion rate is on leads, what it takes to generate the leads in terms of dollars and then based on those number of leads you close, back (divide) in your total marketing and commission and team's cost for helping to close a client/customer. For example, if you generate 100 leads and you only close 10% of the leads and 100 leads cost you, $5,000.00, then if you only close 10% of those leads, it's going to cost you basically $5,000 for those closed leads plus any overhead cost associated with closing those leads. Based on the 100 leads, that converted 10 closed transactions, you divide the 10 leads that you closed into the $5,000 (marketing + commissions + team, etc.) and it cost you $500 per lead or customer acquisition cost. This means that the value of that customer/client needs to be significant to offset your customer acquisition costs. Remember you may have other acquisition costs you need to include so be realistic with all costs associated with acquiring a customer. Here is the point, your customer acquisition cost is very expensive and more so than you probably would estimate and because of that, it's ultimately better to *retain* customers or clients than it is to constantly find new ones.

How do we keep customers? What are the best customer retention strategies and in addition to the notes we have mentioned in this chapter? We are going to give you some examples of clients that we have worked with in addition to our business and how we retain customers. Number one is value! You provide value; value is measured not in terms of dollars spent but in terms of the benefits received for the dollars spent. If the benefits received outweigh the dollar spent the customer sees value and will continue to engage your services or buy your products.

Before we look at driving value, there are a couple different ways you can retain customers; you can look at certain loyalty type programs that help to retain customers by offering discounts, promotions or added services/products for a certain amount of time. If they stay with you for a year, you might discount their year two renewal. If they revisit you, you may discount, or give a 2 for 1 coupon. These strategies for retention are all good and important to consider.

One of the techniques we do in order to provide value is to look at several key opportunities such as birthdays and anniversaries and special holidays. We also reviewed a book called *Giftology* by John Ruhlin and he narrows his strategy down to the fact that providing a gift periodically when it is most unexpected, unique and which that client will appreciate has the most impact. We have done this around the holidays but what *Giftology* talks about is doing it at a time when they <u>don't</u> expect it, not the holidays, birthdays or anniversaries. John Ruhlin also recommends sending gifts to the spouse of your client/customer and even new employees.

We have given custom cutting boards, special books, tickets to special events, etc. I know a group that sends very expensive custom knives. As an example, I recently started a whole new retirement plan and the investment firm sent me some crystal tumblers that were engraved with my initials. These are the types of gifts that you can do that help to show that you care and appreciate their business. Other approaches are simple, open and honest communication on a regular basis, just calling to stay in touch with a client. Taking your customers out to lunch, or sending them communication, positive inspiring quotes, inviting them to webinars or other opportunities. There are more common strategies such as inviting clients to special events or sporting events and those are all great! But a word of caution... remember that you have to be careful, since some customers may not be able to accept a gift because of company policies or regulations. A lot of corporate clients won't accept those, especially publicly traded companies. Giving gifts incorrectly or too frequently may cause your client/customer to expect a gift to show value versus showing value in the services or product you deliver. Try to find value in both the way you deliver services, the way you communicate, and being available and tuned in to your customer needs. The way you show your appreciation for them in just good, common wholesome gestures. Perhaps you wish them a happy birthday and send them a birthday card. Ask if you can take them out to lunch and talk about how you are performing your services. These are just many of the examples that you can look at that will help to retain customers. Again, I want to reiterate you can do it in terms of gifts, which is a value, or you can do it by adjusting the costs of the products or services they spend with you, so that they feel like they have received more value...or you could provide more product or services that is above and beyond what they have expected. Most importantly the goal is to first provide value in your services by delivering 5 star service or products, and then deliver these retention strategies to really wow your customers!

In our case we have continued to serve clients when their cash flow wouldn't permit them to pay our fee. In one case, a client had to pull back on services because their cash flow was tight and we said, "we will continue to provide you the same value of service each week, as if you were paying our normal fee for the next 30 days", and we did this for 60 days until their cash flow improved because we are committed to our client's success for the long haul, and this shows our commitment and the client saw tremendous value. For us, we chose to look at the long term because the cost of acquisition of a new customer and the client's lifetime value is more than the cost of retaining your clients over the long term—and this is always a good strategy to consider!

Retention Strategies Client Spotlight:

Aviation Service & Flight Training School

The aviation company that does pilot flight training was having challenges with losing students who were going through their training. This client needed to increase the retention rate of the students but that was directly tied to the student's ability to pass their different exams in the different stages of training and certifications. What we did was map out those different stages and then we provided incentives to the instructors, to the students and to the advisors for helping students transition through the program at each key stage, and based on percentages of success, the instructors were bonused as well as student advisors, as well as the students who would receive credits that they could use to do actual flight training, (which is what the student's love to do verses just the in class training). This strategy increased the retention rate dramatically and increased the velocity of students moving through their programs, which allowed the school to drive more revenue and improve cash flow. As a result, they were able to promote that the school has a higher pass success and retention rate. Looking from outside, you could not tell that student retention was a critical success strategy. This was far from obvious! You could not see it as a critical interdependency factor.

It took us a few rounds of business impact analysis *(BIA)* to identify the critical linkages that hinge on success or failure of the institution from a customer's standpoint. We explained to the client that "student retention was the oxygen" that enabled the fire to burn. Without oxygen, it does not matter the quality of fuel or wood, there won't be any fire. On the contrary, with an effective supply of oxygen even a poor quality of fuel will burn. Therefore, poor student retention is akin to having smoky environment that reduces effective visibility and respiration. Just as people can choke and die from smoke, so too will the survivability of the institution if student retention was substandard. In other words, retention was synonymous with having or not having goodwill through online reviews on Google Places, Yelp, and Omgili that web-savvy customers use in choosing who deserves their business.

Retention Strategies Client Spotlight:
Commercial Landscape Maintenance Contractor - AZ

We worked with a commercial landscape maintenance company who has to retain properties in order to grow. If they lose a property, the property could be worth $2,000 or $20,000 per month or $24,000 - $240,000 per year. For this customer, we established a property review format where the Account Managers would review and grade the status of their property based on 5 specific areas that were important and that they assessed the Property Managers were monitoring. These areas, if kept up consistently, would ensure the meeting and exceeding the Property Manager's expectations and retention of the property. The Account Managers would report their property status back to their Directors who would review and spot-check to confirm that this is what they saw on the property. The idea was to have the Account Manager proactively identify where a property may be challenged, and they would grade these. We chose a simple color-coded method: RED: The property is on fire or serious trouble, YELLOW: It needs attention and it's getting into trouble, and GREEN: The property is in good shape. If a Director saw that a property was reported as yellow or red they would immediately contact the Account Manager and visit the property to take proactive measures to help improve and modify. If they saw all green, they would still go out and spot-check to confirm for accountability. Trust yet verify.

This system allowed the Directors to oversee the Account Managers performance and also report back to the Property Managers that based on their assessments, this is the status of your property, and do you (Property Manager) see your property in the same way. What that did was to show the Property Managers (their clients), their willingness to proactively assess their performance and communicate to the properties to ensure retention. What this does, is that it reduces the stress and the amount of time needed by the Property Manager. This approach is what I call "removing the thorns" or removing the pain that your client goes through, and they find that when you remove pains in terms of time savings, interruptions, challenges, issues, cost etc., you provide value for your clients and that's what this commercial landscape company did. As a result, their retention rate is very high; they are running at about a 96% to 97% retention rate of all the properties. Which means they incur less cost to grow and grow as a faster pace because they don't have to replace lost properties. We are now setting up retention tracking to further track and identify retention as a key component for the Account Managers and they are bonused on keeping high retention rates, which means they will focus on those areas that ensure retention. High retention allows this client to grow. One of those areas these Account Managers will focus on, is proactive and consistent communication with the Property Managers on a regular basis.

These are examples of retention strategies (and we could write a whole book on just customer retention strategies), but the important point is when you spend the time and money to acquire a customer, take the time and energy to ensure that you get feedback from the customers as to your performance. Secondly, work to provide value in order to retain the customer long term and implement retention strategies. In our consulting business, our average client retention is over 30 months per client because of our results and the high level of trust. Our goal is always to provide value that surpasses what their expectations are, and this is how you generate **Profit by Design.**

Chapter 10
Exit Planning

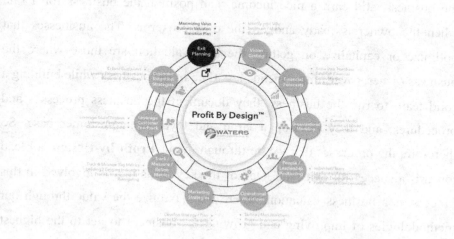

Exit planning is the preparation for the exit or sale of a business owner from his/her company to maximize the value of the company, minimize taxes and plan for other non-financial objectives for a smooth transition.

Exit Planning can include:
- Improving business valuation.
- Maximizing value utilizing business improvement methodologies.
- Transition plan to minimize taxes and maximize owner's gains.

Exit Planning is not a simple transaction that takes place as a one-time event. Exit Planning is a process done over time and with intent. When we work with our clients, we are always in a process of grooming and developing the business such that the business owner can spend less time in the business, still earn a nice income, and position the business for a sale when the owner is ready and on the owner's terms. The businesses that optimize or capitalize on getting the best valuation are those where the business owner, (over time), spends less time in the business while building a solid team to run the business, they document the business processes and procedures, and they develop a large and loyal client/customer base. So therefore, the processes that we go through in our **Profit by Design**, all lead towards a successful exit plan. One of the key areas that is involved in this process, is a business valuation, where we maximize the value through our methodologies of improving and growing the business to get to the highest possible business valuation and then the transition plan.

At WBCG, we strive to help our clients understand that exit strategy planning is like crossing the Pacific Ocean water channel that separates the mainland from San Francisco. We base the strategy partly on the business valuation because business worth sheds light on what strategy will be worth the trouble. In other words, is it worth getting across via the famous Golden Gate Bridge, ferry, train, helicopter, a barge boat, airplane or kayak or horseback? An effective business valuation, enables us to determine issues such as departure time, arrival time, perishability of items, handling, cost of handling, are there any duties, specific excise taxes etc. It also considers other issues such as pending regulations, litigation surrounding the operations.

Our process encompasses every area of Exit Planning and helps to answer the questions business owners have such as:

- What is my business worth?
- How do I determine how much I can get for my business?
- What happens to my employees if I sell my business?
- How do I make my business more valuable or attractive to sell?
- And how much does it cost to sell a business?
- What can I do if I don't want to sell my business, but I also don't want to run the business anymore?
- What should I do if I want the business to be passed to a family member?

As I write this, we are currently going through an exit process with one of our clients. Two partners currently run the business, and one of the partners is presenting an offer letter and agreement to buy out the other partner. In these situations, it is important to go through the process of first accurately calculating the valuation, and then making a fair offer and then establishing the terms. The transaction can be as simple and/or as complex as you make it, but we prefer to try to keep the process straight-forward by being strategic and accomplishing the steps over time. This requires planning well in advance of your exit.

Although I have navigated dozens of business sales, I have also been involved in 8 unique business exit transactions that have helped me to learn what it takes to ensure a successful exit. There is a great book written by John Brown, an attorney who specialized in exit strategy planning called: *How to Run Your Business so You Can Leave it in Style*. His summary is very good, so I pulled from some really good notes and we use them when applicable. A big part of the business exit strategy is understanding it can be a taxable event because capital gains are taxed differently. It is critical to have a strategy in place to protect your income, and to manage that process very effectively to minimize what you pay the IRS.

Some of the things you want to look at when you are leading up to your eventual exit is:

- How to get what you want when you leave or depart the business.
- Valuing your business to maximize what you get but minimize what the IRS takes.
- How to work with professional advisors in the process, not only your Business Consultant but a CPA, an Attorney and Tax Advisors.
- How to create value through your key employees.
- Looking at the best path for departing your business.
- Structuring a business sale for the best benefit of co-owners and employees.
- Selling to a third party or selling to a strategic partner.
- We recommend selling to a strategic partner if possible because they are looking to acquire market share while leveraging your business and their business for accelerated growth and economies of scale, (and they will typically pay more).
- How to leave the business to your children, or other family members.
- Setting up a business continuity agreement.

- How to properly leave the business so that the business continues to succeed upon your departure, especially if you are giving terms to your buyer.

Some of the tax issues that you need to be aware of are minimizing your estate tax and creating a credit shelter to protect you from paying too much in taxes. For these, you want to get the right tax attorney. The keys to successfully selling include determining the amount of income you need annually to secure your financial independence and knowing what that is, defining the type of acquisition terms you would prefer, and then setting a target departure date so you can plan towards that date.

Exit Strategy Client Spotlight:
Carpet & *Flooring Company*

When I started writing this book, we began working with a father and son who own a flooring company. I worked with them in the past and they've re-engaged us recently. During our first meeting they said, *"Our goal is to sell the business and to meet our desired income. We would like to sell the business for about $5 million."* This means they have to grow the business to the point where it's generating enough revenue and profits that the net operating income is somewhere in the neighborhood of $1,250,000 - $1,500,000. This is assuming a buyer will pay a multiple of about 3.5 - 4 times net operating income to get them to about $4,500,000 to $5,000,000.

Ultimately, the valuation is based on EBITDA, (Earnings Before Interest, Taxes, Depreciation, and Amortization). That means those expenses or costs are all part of the due diligence that are looked at in valuing the business. In the case of this flooring contractor, I said, *"Well, let's build a financial model that shows how you are going to get to that number, how we're going to get to the profitability of that number, or EBITDA."* After that, we will need to position the business so that the infrastructure is attractive enough for someone to pay the price tag that the owners want them to pay. I think getting a valuation of 3.5 - 4 could be a stretch, but the way to get there is to get the net profit up higher than a million, five hundred thousand, so that they are guaranteed to get closer to the $5 million they want for the business. In this case, after crunching the numbers, that is our target revenue. We need to generate that $5 million plus in revenue with 15% net profit in order to accommodate both of their lifestyles--so the goal becomes clear, and we can work towards it.

The next thing is to determine the value of the business understanding how the IRS would value the business, so you know what the taxable obligations are. Then, it is important to put together a strong advisory team. It is critical that the right people are on the team, including your attorney, insurance person, financial planner, accountant and tax person. This process requires that every aspect of your current and future finances be looked after!

In addition to your own interest, you will need to look at how to develop programs to retain your key employees. Remember, when you find a good buyer, they will want to know who these key employees are and what the value is that they bring to the business. Make sure that you're leaning on your advisors and don't become an expert yourself. This is certainly a team-effort! Look at the different ways you can actually exit the business and how you want to transfer the ownership, whether it's to a new partner, a strategic buyer or your children. You also want to draw up a continuity agreement; this is critical in order to make sure that the business will succeed upon your departure. But most of all, make sure that your financial planning is in order so that you maximize the dollars you keep and minimize what you pay Uncle Sam.

In the case of the flooring contractor, we are helping them to not only grow their existing store but add two more stores to drive top-line revenue and the net profit to best position them for a successful exit. Multiple locations drive a higher valuation and multiple. So far, we are succeeding, and we are seeing good progress with their growth towards their target of $5 million. During this process, one of the owners said, "now that we're working with you, I want to grow to $10 million...this is fun!" This illustrates, though, that the process of exiting is just that–a process. We do not want to rush, because it is important to be able to get the most out of the business you have worked so hard in!

Exit Strategy Client Spotlight:
Commercial HVAC Company

A few years ago, I worked with a commercial HVAC company where the owner started the business on his own. He had worked for his father and he was going to grow his business so that it could provide a nice income and nest egg for him and his family in the future. A year or so into our engagement, he had an opportunity to sell to a strategic buyer out of Minnesota who came into the Arizona market to expand their service business. I helped him not only clean up his financials and operations to position the company so that the organization structure and the team were intact, I also helped him optimize the valuation at the time of sale. Then I worked with him and the new buyer through the transition to help with a continuity plan as the two cultures and organizations merged their employees and processes to ensure ongoing success. This seller had never been in another business other than his own and his father's HVAC business, so he needed the guidance and the expertise that we brought to the table to help him with the sale of that business, and help him to capitalize on the proceeds. Often business owners don't stay with the new business long because they are so accustomed to running their own business. Many buyers will build in a performance incentive tied to the performance of the business as an incentive to retain the owner's expertise during the business transition. However, our client stayed on with the new buyer for a while, and when he was ready, he opted out and then pursued his dream of traveling with his family for about almost two years.

Exit Strategy Client Spotlight:
Fire & Safety Service and Repair

I am currently working with the two partners who had both talked about selling the business initially when they engaged me. They are in the fire and safety business where they do annual inspections, service inspections, and repairs on deficiencies. Their goal was to eventually sell the business to a strategic buyer (typically a competitor wanting to take on greater market share). However, one of the divisions wasn't performing the way it should, so after our analysis we discussed a strategy to close that division down. I helped them in closing that division, and moving those resources to more profitable areas of the business so we could drive revenues that had higher margins. These higher margins services would drive a higher valuation for the business. The owner's goal is to grow the revenues and margins in the service sector. However, due to poor performance of the one partner in the poor performing construction division, the majority owner recently made an offer to buy out his minority partner. I walked them both through the steps, and advised that the first thing to be done was to determine what they felt was the value of the business. Once you have determined that value, I advised the majority owner to then have the discussion with his partner and let him know that your intention is to buy him out and present a preliminary offer and terms. The majority owner put the offer in a written letter of intent which outlines the offer price, the terms, the timing, etc. The next step we worked on was to allow the minority partner time to review the offer with his legal counsel, and then once they both agree, we move towards the due diligence and prepare the formal documents for the buyout. Currently, the formal documents have been prepared and will be presented to the minority partner to review, and we are walking through that process successfully.

An exit plan can be as unemotional or as emotional as you want it. Many times, business owners have been so intimately involved in their business for so many years that an exit is an emotional event. It is hard for them to give up ownership and pass it along because they birthed the business! You have to make sure that you are ready to make the transition when the time is right. I always recommend that whenever you get into a business, one of the key components is not just how you are going to launch and grow the business, but know how you are going to get out or exit that business. That way you are getting out on your terms and not somebody else's terms. Ultimately, you will exit that business either by health issues or death, by failure due to poor management or economic issues, it could be through divorce or the selling of the business. But by having a plan, then you exit that business on your terms and based on your strategy and timing.

In the example of the flooring business, we are helping to optimize their top-line revenue and their margins to help them get to their selling price in the time they have outlined. They have now gone from wanting out of the business, to enjoying the challenges of growing the business to $10, million instead of $5 million!

In the example of the past commercial HVAC company, we helped them to achieve their exit strategy and gain close to the price they wanted for the business plus acceptable terms and then he worked in the business, with the acquiring entity for a while before pursing his dream and the freedom to travel with his family.

In the situation of the fire and safety business, the majority partner is buying out the other minority partner based on recent valuations that they had received from other strategic buyers that wanted to buy the business earlier in the year. Our client presented a fair offer at a slight discount because they had some losses within the division that was closed down and run by the minority partner. Now the majority partner is excited and energized again to grow the business so that he can optimize the business valuation at an exit based on his timing and terms and then enjoy a life of hunting, fishing and traveling with his family!

Exit Strategy Client Spotlight:
Check Cashing & Title Loan Company

The final Exit Strategy example is about 2 individuals who had a check cashing business. This type of business is a remarkably interesting business model for a variety of reasons. It presents unique challenges with respect to time, space, safety, and significant security concerns. You will see these businesses at corner retail locations where people want to cash their check and they don't have an ID required by a bank. These places will take the risk of cashing your check. The interesting thing in this type of business is the inventory for the business, is cash because you have to have enough cash on hand for people who come in and want to cash checks or borrow money. These companies also do loans, high interest loans. The individuals I worked with were partners and they had a third partner that over time they questioned his integrity because it is a cash business, and there is a lot of cash moving through the business, so they started to lose trust as to what was happening with all the cash. Losing trust is a signal you may want to exit. Besides mistrust, anxiety was creeping up into the spine of the business.

The owners questioned how much money was not being reported and/or stolen? They were uncomfortable continuing to fund the business and they feared potential losses with no way to recover. Such existential concerns keep business owners awake at night. To make matters worse, the owners were feeling distracted from their core business. Obviously, their anxiety and sleeplessness spread to their families and their spouses. This is not a good feeling! Therefore, Owners brought me in to help negotiate an urgent buyout. Time was of essence. Information was of essence. Keeping a tight lip on everything was of essence. Due to the lack of trust and transparency, the owners wanted to eliminate any liability issues that may arise; by selling to the current operator who had interest in buying the Check Cashing stores.

So, I helped them put together a strategy to sell to either of the partners or have the partner buy them out. That was partly the premise of my intervention in the earlier part of consultation. Subsequently, I also helped them with that transition and they successfully exited, and both did very well. The goal was to partly stem the bleeding of mistrust so that they could have the peace of mind to focus on running their business short term.

It's always more comfortable when you are selling a business to work with someone who has done it successfully and can walk you through the steps, if you do it correctly as we have just identified. Done correctly, you ultimately transition out of your business, and you exit successfully, with the price and terms you need to pursue your purpose and passion because you built it and planned for your exit using **Profit by Design Methodologies**.

There's a lot that goes into the planning for selling a business. There's succession planning, decisions on who is going to take over, how to mitigate taxes when receiving the proceeds, do you stay involved for a short period, do you take all cash or terms, etc. If you want to work less, earn more, and be in a position where you can sell a business, that is often what I find a lot of our clients want too. When all was said and done, the transition was relatively seamless because the owners sold to the Operating Manager who had the relationship with the customers and employees. Was it easy? No! Was it impossible? No. It took a proven Exist Strategy that we have used to help clients plan methodically for decades. Today, they are both successful and their family's financial well-being is taken care of for many years, and they don't have the stress and anxiety of questioning the operating partner's trust!

It may be that you're looking for a strategic buyer, one that is wanting to buy the business to grow in the marketplace. It may be just someone moving from the East Coast to the West Coast for a better quality of life or vice versa. Perhaps they just want a business so that they can earn an income and it is more of an investment. In order to determine the best buyer, you need to do a business valuation. We will help to maximize the value of the business through all these processes in our **Profit by Design Methodology** and with a solid transition plan.

Anytime that you sell a business, it's a taxable event, so preparing for it in advance is crucial. This is not only a plan for how you're going to transition yourself, but how you can take care of your employees. Many business owners want the new owners to retain the employees as part of the sale or provide a buy-out. In this way, you can provide incentives for your valued and loyal team. Depending on the type of sale; stock sale, asset sale, partner buyout, ESOP (Employee Stock Owned Purchase), etc. All types of criteria and important points must be included in the discussions when developing the strategy for eventual exit to ensure you maximize your gains, minimize your taxes, and have the best possible terms.

The more you're prepared, the more you're ready when the opportunity comes about. Here's the key: you want to sell your business on your terms. Do not let a life event, divorce or an illness force your hand and catch you unprepared. There are circumstances that can force you out of a business. So, you want to be in control of when (and how) you sell the business…and how you **Profit by Design!**

Conclusion

You may be saying yourself:

- I don't know where to start.
- I need help.
- I don't have the time to add more things to my plate.
- I'm not sure if the plan is going to work.
- Is it too soon to start planning and when is the right time?

Those are all legitimate concerns. But what I will add to that is *action trumps everything*. All goals need to have a strategy designed to achieve them and all strategies need to have action plans with specific details on who will accomplish them and when. When you do this, all actions will ensure the strategy is executed and ultimately you will achieve the goals. Having a consultant, coach, mentor or simply someone who will hold you accountable is a wise decision by you.

As I said earlier, <u>action trumps everything</u> that's why this plan works. What you need to do is to be honest with yourself, and ask, "what is the highest and best use of my time?" Most anything else can be outsourced.

Lastly, remember you are an entrepreneur, you're the founder of the business, you're the owner and CEO and you must continually measure, evaluate and improve. This is ultimately your responsibility, you're the leader of this business. Make the plan and make it happen and take action.

Please feel free to contact us if you have questions or simply need direction with your business.

*If you are interested in learning more about how **Profit by Design** can work for you, or if you simply have questions or need guidance with your business, feel free to contact us at 480.240.1226 or check out our website:*

www.watersbusinessconsulting.com

About the Author:

John Waters

On a Mission to Reach, Teach and Encourage Business Owners

Long before John Waters founded Waters Business Consulting Group (WBCG) based in Scottsdale, Arizona, he was a battle-tested entrepreneur with decades of business experience under his belt. But the story of John Waters doesn't start there.

After college, John co-founded a financial services business in Arizona. With unprecedented success and a lack of self-awareness and alignment with his core values, came shortsightedness in his business practices by both John and his partner. The business collapsed during the 1987 financial crisis and exposed their inexperience and dishonesty. Overnight, John went from being considered a business prodigy to facing public humiliation and serious legal consequences.

Even in the face of such desolation, John refused to exploit any legal loopholes, and he voluntarily faced his challenges and consequences and took ownership. During those dark days, John hit rock bottom. Through a slow process of deep self-reflection, John found a new thread of hope based on his Christian upbringing, values and his determination to find success again—ethically and deliberately. (Look for the full story being written in John's next book, with a working title of, "Overcoming", a story of entrepreneurs and individuals who overcame serious setbacks.)

John was able to move beyond his despair and hopelessness, and from 2000 to 2009, he helped grow a family-owned construction business from $7.5M to $45M. However, success was short-lived. When the Great Recession struck in 2008, the business nosedived to $25M overnight. John and his partners were devastated, but still he did not quit. John rolled up his sleeves and went back to work again. With sheer hard work, sweat, and many sleepless nights, he and his partners repositioned the business on a path to growth and profitability within two years. Today, the company is still flourishing under the leadership of John's brother.

Now, as the President and founder of Waters Business Consulting Group since 2009, John has helped hundreds of business owners attain significant levels of growth and success in business. By combining proven methodologies and techniques, John and his team have coached and supported large and small-scale businesses in the process of scaling up revenues and cash flow, acquiring new customers, and improving operational efficiencies, while reducing operational costs. John knows what it is like to make those tough decisions during turbulent times, and what it takes to ensure profitability without compromising a company's—or personal—values and hard-earned reputation.

In recent years, John decided to start speaking candidly and publicly about his journey from self-destruction, self-examination, and full redemption. More importantly, he continues to feel a profound need to help other business leaders discover the redemptive power of truth in running a successful business with integrity and faith. Increasingly, organizations across the country have sought Johns' advice and his inspirational life lessons to help their teams deal with the pressures of rapid change and disruptions. Over the years, the resonance of his ideas inspired the writing of this book, thanks to suggestions from past and current clients and friends. Unlike some of his competitors without a battle-tested track record, John and his team have spent thousands of hours working in the trenches helping businesses implement plans, strategies, and methodologies that generate ethical profit by design.

In *Profit by Design*, John takes readers into the rough and tumble world of business where tough decisions must be based on a strong foundation of core values and proven methodologies that ensure growth and profitability. Above all, John believes he is on a mission not only to reach and teach but also to 'share' the good news of *Profit by Design*. Without effective design, business owners suffer sudden failures that undermine the jobs, family wellbeing, decades of hard work, values, companies, and millions of dollars. On the contrary, effective design ensures methodical planning and implementation of systems that predicate consistent profit. At best, every business owner will read the success stories in this book; at worse, just one business owner will gain the inspiration to face the trials and tribulations of business with courage. Either way, John believes, he will not rest or stop until he meets that one business owner who needs his message of triumph, encouragement, and faith.

Made in the USA
Monee, IL
27 October 2023